Sacred

*is a Path Book
offering practical spirituality
to enrich everyday living*

*"Your word is a lamp to my feet
and a light to my path."*
Psalm 119:105

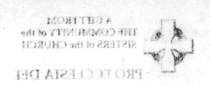

Sacred Simplicities

Seeing the Miracles in Our Lives

Lori Knutson

Path Books

A LIGHT TO MY PATH

ABC Publishing, Anglican Book Centre
General Synod of the Anglican Church of Canada
80 Hayden Street, Toronto, Ontario, Canada M4Y 3G2
abcpublishing@national.anglican.ca
www.abcpublishing.com www.pathbooks.com

Text set in Garamond
Cover and text design by Jane Thornton

Library and Archives Canada Cataloguing in Publication

Knutson, Lori
Sacred simplicities : seeing the miracles in our lives / Lori
Knutson.

ISBN 1-55126-419-6

1. Christian life. I. Title.

BV4501.3.K59 2004   248.4   C2004-904271-8

Contents

Preface

*W*hen I was a kid I discovered a dugout pond hidden in a grove of trees, across a farmer's field from our subdivision in my northern Alberta hometown. It had been a year of new experiences. Just before my discovery, I'd finished reading Mark Twain's *Tom Sawyer*. It was as if my imagination was then born, and with its birth the world took on a different look.

I spent a lot of time alone sitting beside that unused dugout on the bare ground, on a log, or in the crunchy leaves of autumn. Because this favourite place was well sheltered the water was always still, and on sunny days the light would filter down through the trees and dapple everything. In my mind that little pond became the mighty Mississippi, and my head filled with pictures of riverboats and nighttime raft rides designed for escape.

Before too long, I began to explore the entire periphery of the dugout. One day my exploration took me into a thick tangle of bushes almost directly across the green pond from where I did my best daydreaming. It was autumn again, and the leaves lay deep and inviting in various shades of yellow and red. They were deepest directly under the bare mass of branches. So I found a decent-sized hollow between the layer of leaves and the lowest branches, and I burrowed my way in.

For a while I lay still watching the sky — the clouds and the open blue messily latticed by the branches above. Then something lying close by my left hand caught my eye. I grasped it and brought it into my line of sight. It was very light and, upon first examination, appeared to be an ornately carved piece of wood, bleached near-white by seasons of sun and snow. I wondered who would have taken the time to carefully etch so much detail into this brittle wood, including a careful line of what resembled minute teeth....

Aauugghh! A disgusted shudder shook my entire body, as I scrambled up and out of the bush. I tossed the now-recognized rodent skull far from me. All the way home, I felt as if my skin could wriggle its way right off my squeamish frame and stroll along beside me.

Still, even as I shivered and struggled to shake off the heeby-geebies, the story of my experience was forming in my head. By the time I was at the bathroom sink scrubbing my hands clean, the story was almost complete.

I understood then that life and death could not be thought of as separate states; they are necessarily intertwined. As the little woodland creature had died and become part of the landscape, so would I, someday, go back into the earth. This is the fate that I share with the formerly furry little fellow. Such is the cycle of life.

I was about ten or eleven years old when I inadvertently picked up that delicate skull and constructed a story about it. In the same way that this tale was formed, so are the ones you'll discover in the pages of this book — ordinary things and experiences as seen through the imagination that turned a scummy dugout pond into the slowly moving Mississippi River.

How To Use This Book

This is not the sort of book that you must read all the way through, start to finish — although you may do so if you like. The stories need not be experienced in any particular order. You may want to thumb through the book or check the table of contents, and decide where you'd like to start.

The stories may remind you of where you've been, where you are, or where you want to be. As you read, you may notice some connections between your ordinary day and the presence of God. This is the purpose of the book, to help you see the sacred simplicities, the miracles, in your life.

This book can be savoured bit by bit for personal enjoyment — something short to read and ponder when you have a few spare minutes. You might leave it on your coffee table or nightstand, take it with you on a walk in the park, or tuck it into your suitcase to read on the beach or at the cottage on rainy days.

Perhaps you'll want to reflect on the quotations that begin and end each story. You may even check out the Bible or some of the other sources to delve more deeply into the texts.

The book can also be used practically at Bible study meetings, church retreats, or youth group gatherings. If you're preaching sermons, you may choose to quote a story from the book as a real-life example of a point you wish to illustrate.

In the end, how you use this book is up to you. I hope you enjoy it.

Lori Knutson

Seasons
&
Nature

Sky Of Wonder

Psalm 135:5–7

For I know that the Lord is great;
Our Lord is above all gods.
Whatever the Lord pleases he does,
in heaven and on earth,
in the seas and all deeps.
He it is who makes the clouds
rise at the end of the earth;
He makes lightning for the rain
and brings out the wind from his storehouses.

———

*A*s I sit hunched over this keyboard the sun is just breaking through a black wall of clouds, turning the evening lawns green-gold. The pavement shines in its light and hanging branches drip diamonds.

The storm came on suddenly, its crying winds, heavy rains, and hail stones knocking out a clumsy rhythm on our roof and driving the cat to seek refuge under the bed. Then, just like that, it was gone. But while it was here, we shut off the television and watched out the living room window, witnessing slashes of light cross the sky, feeling the shake left by the thunder. It was wonderful. That is, it filled me with wonder.

Watching that storm — gutters rushing, trees bending, hail pellets bouncing off car hoods — I remembered riding in the backseat of my parents' station wagon during a similar cacophony of weather. With my cheek pressed against that cold, cold window, I focused on the charred cloudbank, its edges seared with flame, and imagined God. The Creator had to be there, conducting nature's orchestra, directing the lightning, counting down to the clash of thunder. If I looked hard enough, waited long enough, believed enough, I would know the mystery.

Once upon a time, the sky held an abundance of mystery for

me. There was heaven inhabited by angels, shadows of the dead, and shades of those not yet born. I noticed the gentle shift and change in colour at sunset and would rise early enough to sit on our family's couch, sleepy-eyed and chilled, and see that orange sun break the horizon. The most convincing testimony of God's ability to transform was that nearly imperceptible moment dividing night from morning. That same miracle happened every day when I was a kid.

I suppose it still does, but it's been a very long time since I've noticed. It felt good to see the sky again tonight. I mean, to really see it. As life wears me down, the sky increasingly becomes nothing more than a weather forecast and a fair indicator of the season. Gone is the wonder and gone is the time spent scanning the heavens for the hand of God. Shades of blue run together blandly like whites washed with new jeans, and if I happen to rise early enough to witness the transformation, I choose not to give it my attention.

How would my life be different if once again I could allow the sky its mystery? Nothing's changed between the sky and me since I was a child. I still know virtually nothing about it, would be pressed to tell you even what a cumulus cloud is. The mystery hasn't vanished because of what I've learned or because I've grown up. It's left because I've given it no place to live, denied it shelter and nurturing. It died because I let it.

But perhaps this evening a seed was planted beneath the thunder and lightning. A second chance, a new crop of hope and life. A gift from God in a rain storm and a reminder that life is sweeter when its mystery is recognized.

The most beautiful thing we can experience
is the mysterious.

— Albert Einstein

Snow Day

1 Chronicles 16:11–12

Seek the Lord and his strength, seek his presence
continually. Remember the wonderful works he has done,
his miracles, and the judgements he uttered.

As I walked home from work today I barely recognized the world I inhabit. Within a few days, the blocks surrounding my home that comprise the world I see every day had been transformed. The sinking sun sent gold and blue streaks shimmering across the surface of the new-fallen snow, and the bare branches, formerly light and carefree, now carried the weight of their winter's burden. Snow tires on passing cars spun up bits of sandy snow, and my steps crunched along the unshovelled sidewalk. The laughter of children, happy to be home and playing, lost its shrillness all wrapped up and muffled by layers of snowsuit.

And the kids weren't the only ones bundled against the snow. As I trudged home, my nylon snowpants swished to the rhythm of my stride and I felt that I could easily be mistaken for a close relative of the turtle in my bulky, down-filled jacket and vision-obscuring hood. My hands, clumsy in unfamiliar mitts, clutched the briefcase handle they couldn't actually feel but knew had to be there as the briefcase went where I did.

External factors do much to influence our internal workings. Today everyone I met was tired. I attributed the sleepiness to the rapidly falling temperatures, the banking snow, and what I believe is our natural inclination to hibernate with the onset of this kind of weather. With the beginning of winter our body rhythms seem to change. But another less physical, more subtle change also takes place — or at least it does for me.

As I walked through that suddenly cold, newly-beautiful world, something that had lain dormant in me for a little less than a year awoke to life. I recognized it immediately but, as usual, was surprised by its return. How can something so sweet, so pure come back to me year after year, strangely untainted and tasting fresh no matter what trials the year before held?

Those memories of winters past — scrambling over the towering, dirty snow ridge that the grader had left down the middle of main street, falling into snow I trusted enough to catch me and making an angel, attending a candlelit church service and knowing for sure that a Saviour was born — with each year's first snowfall they greet me anew, bringing with them the childhood excitement of the promise of Christmas, toboggans, cookies and milk, as if each flake holds a particle of hope. All my life, that new snow has meant hope. As my fondest memories are recreated, I am reminded of the potential for re-creation in my own life, in my community, and in the world.

Sure, along with the snow come frosty windshields and frosty fingertips. The roads become icy and sometimes impassable, and getting anywhere is an adventure. But even as I shove my disobedient shopping cart through the snow toward my frozen car, a single snowflake lands on the cart handle right between my mittens and in it I see a future full of promise.

I see the snow as one of God's gifts of hope to us and a reminder of all that has been good and will be again. The snow brings to life memories of joy and reminds us of the blessing of being alive to witness it once more whitening the landscape.

———

And beauty is not a need but an ecstasy.
It is not a mouth thirsting nor an empty hand stretched forth,
But rather a heart enflamed and a soul enchanted.

— Kahlil Gibran, "The Prophet"
from *Gibran's Masterpiece*

Soul Satisfaction

Psalm 104:10–13

You make springs gush forth in the valleys;
They flow between the hills, giving drink to every wild
animal;
The wild asses quench their thirst.
By the streams the birds of the air have their habitation;
they sing among the branches.
From your lofty abode you water the mountains;
the earth is satisfied with the fruit of your work.

———

We just got back from vacationing in British Columbia's Okanagan country, where the sun shone constantly and where I was rejuvenated. We drove west from Calgary into the Rocky Mountains at Banff National Park, unsure how to answer the smiling, bilingual man in the rustic booth with the flashing light. "Will you folks be stopping in the park?" Is getting fuel considered stopping? Pulling over to gawk at a goat? Using a roadside restroom?

After a long, uncomfortable pause during the course of which we considered these and other scenarios we told the nice man that, no, we would not be stopping. Half an hour later, we felt pretty guilty cruising into the Banff town site to buy mints and hoped desperately that the mountain park police wouldn't catch us and try to take away our candy. Fortunately they did not, and all too soon we were through the park.

So many years had passed since I had made that trip through Roger's Pass that I'd somehow forgotten (although now it seems impossible) the resplendent beauty of those great masses of rock carved out by God, framed by the brilliant blue of July sky, their rough and smooth surfaces lit by the sun. Seeing them again raised up a strange sensation somewhere inside. Was it in my heart, in my veins, in the pit of my stomach? I couldn't tell. But whatever it was, it felt good. Really good.

As I guided our car through tunnels under the railway tracks, the feeling grew. With each tunnel it grew a little more, and it kept on growing as the mountains gradually spread and opened up into a sprawling valley with sapphire lakes deep as oceans. Both mornings when we were in Vernon, we ate at an orchard café overlooking the little city and the lands surrounding it. There I sat in the shade of a willow tree, drinking dark roasted coffee and thinking this place was paradise. And at the thought, the feeling grew again. By now, it felt like the core at the centre of who I am.

Although I thought there was no room left for growth, the feeling surprised me repeatedly with tiny bursts of growth along our return journey. It surprised me at a roadside café with a history of murder, caught me off guard on two ferry rides, startled me as I sank into the pristine waters of the Nakusp hot springs, and dazzled me while we hiked beneath stretching cedar branches.

By the time we reached home, I was tired from the long drive but the feeling hadn't faded; in fact, it seemed stronger than ever. It was while driving into the city that I realized how long it had been since I had revelled in the glory of God's creation and taken time to soak in the energy it provides. The mystery of the feeling was solved. Finally I understood.

My soul had gone without water for so long, I'd forgotten I was thirsty; my heart so long without joy, I'd not remembered I was sad. In the wonders of God's creation I was replenished, blessed to overflowing by the miracles of the earth. The Creator had seen my soul hungry for beauty, knew its craving for life's sweetness, and so replenished my spirit. I was satisfied.

Nothing divine dies. All good is eternally reproductive. The beauty of nature reforms itself in the mind, and not for barren contemplation, but for new creation.

— Ralph Waldo Emerson

Weather Talk

Psalm 74:16–17

Yours is the day, yours also the night;
you established the luminaries and the sun.
You have fixed all the bounds of the earth;
you made summer and winter.

———

*L*ately everywhere I turn I'm hearing and making comments about
the unseasonably cool weather. It feels as though spring will never
arrive. The world seems not to be thawing out. The leaves are reluctant to open and the flowers scared to grow. Glancing out my window I
can see that the hearty grass has voted to turn green in more-sheltered
areas, and I'm proud of it for taking that step. Hopefully, its model of
bravery will encourage other plant life to do the same.

Our conversations are filled with comments on the weather: Cold
enough for you? Hot enough for you? Will this wind ever stop? Well,
I guess we've had our summer. We need the moisture. In Canada,
talk of the weather is a constant theme, and I pray that it will continue to be.

Why? Because I am enthralled by weather talk and couldn't survive without a daily dose of it? Or because I fear that human
interaction in Canada would end completely if we no longer opened
conversations with weather talk? No, it's neither.

The reason is this: When the weather is our problem, our problems are small.

A writer in published disagreement with the government in power
does not notice whether or not it is snowing beyond his vermin-
infested prison cell. He may sometimes dreams of images of the sky
and pray that one day he may again see it for himself.

A woman beaten and raped in a downtown alley way doesn't feel
the rain streaming down her bruised and swollen face as she lies half-
conscious and vulnerable in the light of early dawn. When an elderly

woman's village is burned to the ground because her sons voted for the wrong party in her country's first "free" election, she doesn't look ahead to what kind of weather the monsoon will bring as she buries her dead. She throws her head back and wails her rage and grief without seeing the sky. In fact, she may cry her eyes blind and never see it again.

As long as we're "talkin' weather," it's a sign that we can feel the icy wind or the warm sun or the snowflakes in May. When one farmer asks another in the grocery store, "Cold enough for you?" there's probably no war in his country and no genocide or torture taking place nearby.

Hearing talk about the weather makes me feel fortunate to live where weather is such a big consideration and famine and war are not. But it also leaves me with heavier thoughts of those who don't discuss the weather as often. Perhaps I'll try to whisper a prayer for those suffering people each time I mention the weather. It's the least I can do in my little life, where scraping a layer of frost from my windshield is an inconvenience and rain on a long weekend, a disaster.

⸺

When I hear somebody sigh, "Life is hard," I am always tempted to ask, "Compared to what?"

— Sydney Harris

Our Joy Is God's Joy

Ecclesiastes 8:7–8

Go, eat your bread with enjoyment, and drink your
wine with a merry heart; for God has long ago approved
what you do. Let your garments always be white; do not let
oil be lacking on your head.

---

*A*s soon as I got back from the library I sat down at the computer
to write this article for my newspaper. I'd completely forgotten
about it. Instead I was traipsing about, seeking fiction and recently
released magazines, thinking all the while, "What a beautiful day!"

That's summertime for you. The shackles and constraints of routine fall away, allowing us to temporarily lose track of obligations and
responsibilities. Life is lighter, worries weigh less, vacation time makes
work feel distant, and fun and relaxation become the priorities.

Some of us even research our fun, not wanting to miss out on a
golden opportunity to do something exciting and/or interesting simply because we were poorly informed. We scan with intensity the
road maps and travel guides spread over picnic tables, kitchen tables,
patio tables, fold-down tables in campers and motor homes.

In summer we search for restaurants boasting outdoor patios with
huge umbrellas and baskets of hanging flowers. We bring our canoes,
fishing rods, and tents to the often algae-infested puddles that dot
our prairie landscape and do duty as lakes in the summertime. There's
music and magic at festivals across the country, pretty dresses and
hemp jewelry at sidewalk sales, parades and parties at weekends.

At other times of the year, I like to get out and walk, but during
the summer I *love* it. There's nothing like moving along a shady
sidewalk in some small town or in a city subdivision, and breathing
in deep the scent of lilacs, petunias, freshly-mowed lawn, and roses.
It's the only time of the year you'll catch me eating hotdogs and drinking beer from frosted mugs.

All these many pleasures — the sunshine, the food, the travel, the social times — cause me to wonder why we don't treat life with similar enthusiasm for the rest of the year. Why can't that same lightness of heart be transported into February? Surely snowflakes drift as easily as dandelion down or poplar fluff, and isn't the winter sun reflecting off the snow at noon as bright as the summer sun in June? I can't tell if the reasons why our moods change with the seasons are internal or external: do our attitudes come first, or do the seasons bring with them certain emotions?

But never mind that now. It's summer. And the author of Ecclesiastes tells us that before we were born, God approved of our enjoyment of life. So go ahead! Drink your wine, eat those hotdogs, trace your finger down the side of that frosted mug, and inhale the sweet scents of summer, remembering that from your joy also springs the Creator's.

———

Be happy while you're living, for you're a long time dead.

— Scottish proverb

Blessed With Nasal Congestion

Job 37:6–10

For to the snow he says, "Fall on the earth"; and the shower
of rain, his heavy shower of rain, serves as a sign on
everyone's hand, so that all whom he has made may know
it. Then the animals go into their lairs and remain in their
dens. From its chamber comes the whirlwind, and cold from
the scattering winds. By the breath of God ice is given, and
the broad waters are frozen fast.

I woke up this past Monday morning with a full-blown cold. There's
a good reason for it, too, and I need to accept responsibility for
this one. Instead of relaxing on Friday evening and during the weekend when I felt the cold coming on, I decided to enjoy a roaring
social life even though I knew the penalty would be congestion and
mild aches accompanied by low energy.

As I moved from friend to friend and from one fun situation
into another, it was as if I were being pursued. I took a moment
(albeit a short moment) to figure it out. I *am* being pursued — we all
are. Winter is hot (or is it cold?) on our tails and some of us are
illogically trying to outrun it or to at least squeeze as much enjoyment as we can out of before the snow falls and temperatures plunge.

Over that weekend I was trying to run fast enough both to escape the coming cold and to chase down and capture the last few
days of our short northern autumn. It's true that I ended up with a
cold, but I had a blast in the meantime! Was it worth a runny nose
and stuffy head? Completely.

As the bitter wind tears the withered leaves from grey dry branches
and drives right through your flesh and into your bones, it's sometimes hard to see the rapid onset of winter as a blessing. But I

recognized it as such in my sudden zest for life on that cold-causing weekend. I don't think I could have appreciated my friends, the food, the drink, or the music in quite the same way without knowing that winter is waiting only a few steps away to freeze me in my tracks. Indeed, focusing on the time that is now takes the bitterness out of the dropping temperatures so that even the present tastes sweeter.

We live in a country where God's breath is evident in the dramatic change of seasons. This can serve as a reminder of life's brevity, of the gift of change, and of the ever-onward flow of time. All of these are blessings. Life's finiteness leaves us craving the next day and caressing the memory of times past that touched and formed us. Change tells us that every day can be a new start; even though we lose the things we loved, more love waits down the road.

I owe my glorious weekend and my nasal congestion to the change of seasons and to God's breath moving through my life, always challenging me to taste life in all its flavours and colours. The whole experience has left me feeling more grateful for those hard pellets of falling snow than I ever thought I could.

Experience is not what happens to you —
it's how you interpret what happens to you.

— Aldous Huxley

The Call

Psalm 102:1–2

Hear my prayer, O Lord;
let my cry come to you.
Do not hide your face from me
in the day of my distress.
Incline your ear to me;
answer me speedily in the day
when I call.

We heard him before we saw him, his crazy cry echoing from over the pines and poplars and across the tiny, greenish, man-made lake in northern Alberta lake. The call compelled us to paddle our red canoe straight toward his voice and within a few minutes, the loon was in sight.

Early in the morning, about the same time the sun begins its long trek across the July sky, he beat the surface of the smooth water, breaking it into splashes from which tiny ripples extended outward for several metres before subsiding into stillness again. His dance was comical yet methodical in its definite rhythm and pattern. He swam like a duck for a little way, dove suddenly, then rose from the water with what seemed like a mixture of jubilation and desperation, so high that his feet tap-danced on the water's surface while his wings flapped wildly. It was during this walking-on-water routine that he sang his high, quavering song. Then the dance began again: the calm swimming followed by the dive and finally the exuberant strut upon the water.

In the canoe we were able to tail him all around the lake, and he showed little concern or even interest. After all, it wasn't a couple of canoeists puffed-up in their bright orange lifejackets that he was looking for. It was a girlfriend he sought.

Not long after we heard his initial call and located him, a voice answered from the other side of the trees surrounding the lake. He seemed to dive deeper, flap harder, and call louder. Again his call was returned. The owner of the voice seemed nearer this time, but she had not yet come into view. Then unexpectedly another voice joined the tremolo chorus. Apparently the male loon's antics had attracted the attention of another female.

Within moments both ladies had joined their suitor on the water, and all three danced and splashed and played while we watched from the canoe, feeling blessed to witness this frolicking, and at the same time feeling our unimportance to these beautiful lunatics, who completely ignored our presence.

The loons reminded me of my sometimes poor attempts at prayer. Often short, heartless, and without real faith that I'll receive an answer, they're more an attempt to console myself than to seek spiritual union with the Almighty. I wonder how pleasing these shallow endeavors are to God? They're certainly not the festive, joyful, hopeful display put forth by the loons, who seem to know why they were created and what capacity they hold for feeling and giving joy.

Perhaps the joy is the key. To both experience it and give it generously.

The loon gave me hope that in my sometimes desperate dance to seek and speak with God, my voice will not go unheeded as long as I just keep on dancing. Eventually, if I put in the time and energy and perhaps a touch of creativity, a voice from over the pines and poplars and across the greenish lake will surely answer.

Every joy is gain,
and gain is gain, however small.

— Robert Browning

Light To Our Dark

Luke 11:33–36

No one after lighting a lamp puts it in a cellar, but on
the lampstand so that those who enter may see the light.
Your eye is the lamp of your body. If your eye is healthy,
your whole body is full of light; but if it is not healthy, your
body is full of darkness. Therefore consider whether the light
in you is not darkness. If then your whole body is full of
light, with no part of it in darkness, it will be as full of light
as when a lamp gives you light with its rays.

———

Finally the first warm day of spring is upon us. The sun's warmth
penetrates even the gale-force wind we've nearly gotten used to
and accepted as normal. Suddenly tree branches viewed from a distance show a light green haze. Upon closer inspection it becomes
apparent that the mysterious glow is actually thousands of sticky buds
opening and growing simultaneously. Everywhere millions of green
shoots poke up through the dusty soil promising lush growth, and
out of their houses come the people, blinking hard against the unfamiliar light, to shake the dust from their souls.

Out come the bedding plants, the trampolines, and the lemon-
ade. Cyclists, rollerbladers, joggers, and dog-walkers fill the sidewalks
and paths with their energy and optimism. For northern people the
arrival of spring affirms our optimism, tells us that it's safe to hope
because spring does indeed return. People smile and greet one another easily.

As I stroll down residential streets with the warm sun on my
back, I hear neighbours chatting over lawnmowers and potting soil.
It sounds less like idle chatter than interactions between lonely spirits who have craved this type of connection all winter long and are
now finally meeting beneath leafing branches and a clear blue dome
sky. The whole world seems instantly happier.

Walking along, watching, and doing my own interacting with these folks, I get to thinking about how something external like a sudden change in the weather steers us in a new direction. When the sun is out, and once again we see our neighbours and feel the young grasses bend beneath our bare toes, we are guided in the direction of good naturedness toward the people around us and toward all of creation.

But at other times we give over control to more negative external factors. Often if someone is inadvertently or purposefully rude to us in the morning, we carry a bitter feeling around until evening; really, it would be in our best interest to let that feeling go at lunchtime! And just as the sunny weather brings us lightheartedness, cloudy, cool weather can quickly dampen the most boisterous of spirits.

I wonder why we are affected so strongly by what lies outside us. Is the internal not as present as the external? Is it not as strong, not as rewarding? Do we give what lies on the inside less of our attention? I guess I'm just wondering whether the light within me may be darkness or whether it couldn't at least be brighter.

Then when things aren't going so well and the weather is cloudy, perhaps I would find inner strength. Maybe I would call up my neighbours to come and play cards one winter evening.

That sunshiny spring day made me think that it's too bad we can't treat each other like old friends everyday. It's too bad that we can't always feel that lightness in our steps and that flutter in our hearts just because we're alive. But this can only happen when the internal is given more control than the external, when the light in our bodies fills us and beckons to those around us, even when the sun is not out and the snow lies a foot deep on the ground. Then our kindness and connection to one another will be assured, not by the season but instead by our own shining souls.

Just when you think that a person is just a backdrop for the rest of the universe, watch them and see that they laugh, they cry, they tell jokes …
they're just friends waiting to be made.

— Dr. Jeffrey Borenstein

Riches Don't Last Forever

Proverbs 27:23–27

Know well the condition of your flocks,
and give attention to your herd;
for riches do not last forever,
nor a crown for all generations.
When the grass is gone, and new growth appears,
and the herbage of the mountains is gathered,
the lambs will provide your clothing,
and the goats the price of a field;
there will be enough goats' milk for your food,
for the food of your household and nourishment for your
servant-girls.

———

I guess you could call it eavesdropping because it was conversation not involving me, but I couldn't help listening. The topic reached out and grabbed my attention: farming. This conversational exchange didn't put farming in the best light. The two women talking were telling one another about how each had discouraged a family member (one a husband, the other a son) from becoming a farmer for two obvious and practical reasons: it's very hard work for which you get very little money.

Yet under their words I could sense the sadness at something lost, like mourning someone you didn't know but wish you had. Then one of the women said, "You just can't do it anymore. It's impossible unless someone's given you a farm." The sadness had risen to the surface — and not just in her words, but also in the eyes of those listening and in their slow, sombre nods.

What were we, the participants and the eavesdroppers, feeling so suddenly melancholy about? It sounds trite, but I'll risk saying it. We were mourning the loss of a way of life that likely won't return in our lifetimes. We'd all seen some of it, many of us had lived it. Some of us had grown up on the family farm, others of us had had grandparents who worked on the land. It wasn't planned that Canadians would stop living that way. Things just changed and life went in a different direction as life does. We of course went with it, and the old ways were gone.

We're urban folk now, buying eggs and chickens that rest perfectly on Styrofoam in the supermarket cooler, and bread and cookies fresh from the shelf. Fruits and vegetables that used to be only available "in season" can now be purchased any old time of the year and they last forever — like mummies. They look good on the outside, but what was pumped into them to make them immortal?

We have quickly moved from being a people aware of our dependence upon the land to being a generation living as if land were just a space to build a box store, and as if all we'll need to survive will spring forth spontaneously from immense tiled floors below blinding halogen lights.

In those moments when we realize that we'll not live as farmers again, do we also realize what an important tie has been severed? Being removed from nature and being the masters of technology gives us a false sense of immunity in the developed urban world. When we fall out of touch with God's creation and gain so much control over the earth, it's easy to forget that we are dependent upon the soil and the sun for our survival. The truth is that, although we've created a technology to maneuver nature, we're not the makers of the planet that sustains us. Our technology can't replace or replenish what we're gobbling up. Perhaps we're out of touch with the condition of our flocks and would do well to heed Proverbs: "Riches do not last forever, nor a crown for all generations."

———

To cherish what remains of the Earth and to foster its renewal is our only legitimate hope of survival.

— Wendell Berry

Hear the Tiger Lilies Roar

Ecclesiastes 11:3–5

When clouds are full,
they empty rain on the earth;
whether a tree falls to the south
or to the north,
in the place where the tree
falls, there it will lie.
Whoever observes the wind will
not sow;
and whoever regards the clouds
will not reap.

Just as you do not know how the breath comes to the bones
in the mother's womb, so you do not know the work of God,
who makes everything.

―――

The other day a friend and I went for a hike. Trees both decidu-
ous and coniferous stretched tall, reaching for the sun on either
side of the path that was sometimes narrow, often wide, and constantly unfamiliar. On the forest floor alongside the trail, delicate
white flowers signalled the coming of wild strawberries. Tiger lilies,
smaller than their domestic cousins, burst from the green in shots of
orange, surprising passers-by with their unabashed colour. Bluebells
and purple flowers to whom I've never been formally introduced stood
prettily and proudly where the sunbeams could reach them, while
other smaller flowers and several low green plants covered the earth
where the sun doesn't often find its way.

Birds sang and, though we couldn't see the woodland creatures,
we saw evidence that they were not far away — maybe even watching
us from the cover of forest. Through the canopy of treetops, patches
of clear blue sky glinted cheerfully, and for the duration of the short
walk, the world in that place and time seemed perfect.

Then my mind turned to melancholy thoughts. (Why can't I just lighten up and enjoy a walk?) Everything in creation that lies in its glory around us will soon be gone. With the fall, the roof of leaves will yellow and tumble to the ground to crinkle and decay. In a couple of short weeks, those wild orange tigers will lose their vibrant colour and the ability to startle anyone. Bluebells will cease their ringing and I will mourn the passing of the purple flowers I never learned the names of. Every bird that sings in the trees will die; every person who walks through the woods will meet the same fate.

It is natural to lament that everything created fades and dies. But perhaps the point is the beauty of the moment, and the miracle is that any of it existed at all. Awareness of everything's mortality makes us notice and appreciate. It makes us savour and taste and listen with our souls to the music of creation — unless, of course, we choose to dwell on the death and not the life. In that case, everything created becomes in our eyes just something waiting for its turn to die.

Babies grow old, but there is magic in their special smell and in their soft skin and in their large, searching eyes. What a sad thing it would be if, upon the birth of an infant, all we could consider was its death. Thankfully, it's the moment of life's arrival that catches us, that leaves us wondering at the mystery of this always temporary gift.

Moments full of life and beauty are islands in the sea of sorrow of impending death. We have a choice: we may swim in death or choose life on the islands; spiritually drown or seek the sands of hope. I came out of the woods knowing that the tiger lilies will soon die, but I am blessed to have heard them roar at all.

The tragedy of life is not that it ends so soon,
but that we wait so long to begin it.

— W. M. Lewis

Connectedness

Time Well Wasted

Sirach 7:36

In all you do, remember the end of your life, and then you will never sin.

Not so long ago I was having a casual conversation with a good friend. I asked her, "So, what'd ya do this morning?"

"I wasted the whole morning! I was planning to clean out my storage room and take in my recycling. Instead I spent time on the phone with three different friends I hadn't talked to in a long time."

My response was something like this: "Yeah, now your storage room will be untidy, but at least three people will come to your funeral."

I was in the position to gently tease my friend about what she considers to be "a waste of time" because I've often felt the same way about spending time with the people I love instead of getting really important stuff done. I've caught myself thinking while cooking a meal or while playing a game of yahtzee over a bottle of red wine or endless cups of coffee, "I really should be writing or planning or cleaning or …."

How much more misguided could I possibly be? In the end, all that's going to matter is that I spent the time connecting with others in a loving way. That's it. That's all. That's everything. Yet I fret about things ultimately have no meaning.

It's unlikely that when I arrive at those Pearly Gates, surprised to have died in the way I did or even to have died at all, St. Peter will greet me, commenting, "We'd like to let you in, Ms. Knutson, but upon scheduling your arrival, we checked your closet and found a couple of rather large dust bunnies waltzing with your shoes. We probably could've let that pass but then we checked your computer's hard drive and discovered that you did not, after all, edit that short story you wrote five years ago, let alone send it out to the magazine.

How do you expect us to ignore behaviour like that? Surely you must understand that we cannot, under any circumstances, allow slouches into Heaven. Now, take your yearly museum pass, game boards, and long-distance calling plan and be off with you."

Instead, it's the love and the connections that will be remembered and taken into consideration by those left behind.

Here's something I just remembered. A couple of times each year, I get a card from an old friend of my grandmother, and she never fails to mention what a great housekeeper Grandma was and how tidy she kept her yard. It's nice that Evy thinks these kind thoughts about my beloved grandma, but how I long to open a card that says, "One time, my husband really hurt my feelings and I knew I could turn to your grandma to listen and to console me when I felt very alone. She could be counted on to keep a confidence and to carry on as if nothing had ever happened after my better half and I patched things up."

Maybe — likely — my grandma was a good and true friend to be leaned on, but I yearn to hear it said. It doesn't matter to me that she ironed and starched her tablecloths and pruned the raspberry bushes. I want to know that she loved and was loved in return.

What my telephone-talkin' friend and those occasional greeting cards have taught me is that life is too short not to "waste" time on forming meaningful relationships, that dust bunnies can wait and once eradicated will only be born again, that full pews at my memorial service may someday mean more than no crumbs in my cupboards.

Be good and you will be lonesome.

— Mark Twain

Something We All Have
In Common

Genesis 3:19

By the sweat of your face you shall eat bread until you
return to the ground,
for out of it you were taken; you are dust, and to dust you
shall return.

————

*Y*esterday I made the long journey to visit a meaningful cemetery
that lies dry and dusty just outside an isolated northern community a couple of hours' drive from where I live. As usual, it wasn't a
trip I particularly wanted to make, so with little enthusiasm I gassed
up my car and hit the open road in the glaring mid-afternoon sunshine. The time at the cemetery was thinking time, memory time, a
time to pull it all together and try to make sense of why exactly we're
here, and where the time goes that passes so quickly, leaving us dead
as ashes as it dashes on. (Cheerful, I know, but it's a cemetery story.
What'd you expect?)

Beside me on the passenger seat rested a gift for the dead: an
elegant paraffin lamp made of thick glass and filled with somehow-
preserved roses. Maybe when someone comes to pay a visit, they'll
light it for a moment of remembrance. That's what I was hoping,
anyway. On the floor of the back seat lay a broom and some clippers
to thin the dandelions and dust the marble surfaces.

The drive tired me out. so when finally I stepped from my little
car, it was on wobbly legs that I made my way across the crab grass
and struggling wild flowers. My visit was short, perhaps fifteen or
twenty minutes, but long enough to do what needed to be done, to
say what needed to be said, and to pray what needed to be prayed. I
can't say I was happy or comforted, but I have to admit feeling a
connectedness to a part of my life I had sorely neglected.

As I swept and pondered there alone in the heat, a red-tailed hawk flew in loose loops high above, came in closer for a bit (probably to ascertain whether or not I'm small enough to be lunch) and then slowly ascended, circling silently and moving higher until out of sight. What a blessing was this graceful guest, for he brought me hope and lightened my heavy thoughts of death.

The hawk reminded me of how the dead may interact with us from a distance when we choose to remember and include them in the continuance of our own short lives. Like the predatory bird, they come close for a bit but mostly stay out of our sight.

In a way it's a shame that our Western culture tends to set the dead aside and pay them little heed. We have almost nothing to do with burial rites, handing that task over to professionals who bathe and dress and lay out those whose souls have departed. We've neatly separated ourselves from the dirty realities of death, sterilized the entire process, cleaned it up and packaged it tidily, but at what expense to our own souls? Do we cry out silently for our dead, not knowing how to express our grief or even if it's acceptable to do so? I wonder, do our attempts to separate ourselves from the dead leave us feeling more isolated from both them and the living for remainder of our lives?

It had probably been two years since I had last visited this cemetery. Even if the dead are not aware that we miss and love them still, showing that I do gives further balance and fullness to my life. Yes. Death is messy and heart-wrenching and inevitable. Perhaps in its acceptance and inclusion in life, I'll be able to find a connectedness I'd otherwise miss.

The same stream of life
That runs through my veins
Night and day
Runs through the world
And dances in rhythmic measures.

— Rabindranath Tagore

No Fear, No Trust

Psalm 40:4

Happy are those who make
the Lord their trust,
who do not turn to the proud,
to those who go astray after false gods.

———

"*I* have no fear."

That's what one of my newest acquaintances told me while we were discussing his unconventional future plans and I thought, "Hmmm ... no fear, eh? How very unnatural." But I didn't say it. I just smiled and nodded, not wanting to break the reverie he was experiencing in talking about himself. (I know, I know. Who of us can't be said to enjoy talking about ourselves from time to time? But, I swear, that was the only topic of conversation in this guy's repertoire.)

No fear. We see it everywhere. On television ads, on T-shirts, and baseball caps worn jaunty and backwards, in the rear windows of shiny pick-ups and fast cars. It boasts, I suppose, no fear of tackling life and its challenges head-on with complete confidence of being the victor on any battlefield. I don't know about you, but I have a real hard time relating to someone who wins all the time ... probably because that's just never been my experience with life. A wise person once said, "What can ya do? Ya win some, ya lose some." That's much truer to my personal trek through the day to day.

What's more, I have trouble even liking a person with no fear and a driving need to win all the time. Who wants to be around someone like that? If they're always the winner, what does that make you? If their shirt reads "No fear," yours will certainly say, "No trust." Not much of a basis for a friendship.

Another closer friend made an interesting observation regarding her young children. "They are born without fear." She went on to say that she wishes they were born with a little fear so that they wouldn't climb so high, run out into the street, talk to strangers. As a mother, she views a touch of fear as a guardian for her kids in helping them to make safe choices. My friend is able to see where some fear can benefit her kids while at play and can generally ease her mind as a parent.

Our fearlessness as children results from our obvious lack of life experience. As we live, most of us gain fear, regardless of what the slogan in the back window of our Ford Tempo may read. We love, our hearts get broken, and so inevitably we are afraid to love again.

A woman driving her car is involved in a horrific accident that takes another's life, and for the next six months she lets her husband drive everywhere. A man in Tokyo on business is stuck in an elevator on the thirty-third floor for two hours during an earth tremor. For the remainder of the trip, he takes the stairs.

We live, we learn fear. This doesn't mean we walk around scared all the time. It simply means that we've learned the lesson that it sometimes hurts to really live. This leads me to believe that those who claim to have no fear must be life virgins, fearless as newborns because they've dared not live.

The really brave ones are those who have lived life, fallen down, suffered broken bones and broken hearts, and continue living — but now with fear to warn them and faith to keep them moving forward. Fear is a gift. Feeling it is human. Like any God-given emotion, it can rule us. But it doesn't have to. Dealing with it requires faith that we are born to live and hurt and fear and then to keep on going, more tentatively sometimes, but still discovering the joys God has in store for us.

I think that in many cases people tend to expect the other person to respond to them in a positive way first, rather than taking the initiative themselves to create that possibility. I feel that's wrong; it leads to problems and can act as a barrier that just serves to promote a feeling of isolation from others. So, if you wish to overcome that feeling of isolation and loneliness, I think that your underlying attitude makes a tremendous difference. And approaching others with the thought of compassion in your mind is the best way to do this.

— The Dalai Lama from *The Art of Happiness*

Home Preserving Tips

Proverbs 30:17

The eye that mocks a father
and scorns to obey a mother
will be pecked out by the ravens
of the valley
and eaten by the vultures.

—◦—

$\mathcal{T}$he other day I was going through some stuff. The mystery boxes in my cluttered storage room were full of junk placed there long ago when I still thought of it as treasure. A coffee can of pennies, a Mason jar of potting soil (over five years old and, boy, did it reek!) jars of expired beet pickles and deceased jellies, a jug of formerly white vinegar long since yellowed, bits of fabric and yarn too small for any use besides lining a bird's nest or housing baby mice.

Among all of these crucial treasures was a smaller box designed to hold twelve 250-ml jelly jars. On its outside, printed in thick white lettering against a red background were these thought-provoking words: "home preserving jars." Ahh. If only it were that simple.

Dad's not listening to Mom and the TV's blaring. "Son, fetch a jar of attentiveness from the pantry, would you? I'm feeling unloved and unimportant with your father ignoring me in this way."

A fed-up mom is about to kick her teenage son out of the house for good, when Grandma comes strolling up the sidewalk with a couple jars of patience and foresight she cooked up just that morning from a special recipe containing a hint of unconditional love. Two sisters continually call one another down, picking at looks, weight, and personality flaws until Dad reaches into the back of the fridge where he's sure he spotted a nice compassion and understanding chutney last week.

Unfortunately, it isn't that easy. Living with people can be hard work. Living alone has its drawbacks as well. So home preserving is not consistently easy, no matter in which situation you may find yourself. I think successful home preservation lies in seeing another person's point of view even if you're not able to always agree with it (because that's just plain unrealistic), and living alone in a home requires being contented (most of the time) with your own company and developing the ability to ward off inevitable loneliness.

For the most part we've given up telling disobedient children that the ravens will peck out their eyes — the proverb seems a little outdated. (By the way, how come the vultures get to eat the eye after the ravens went to all the work of plucking it out?) In those times suppression was thought to be the best way of managing the household. Even now, few would disagree that homes function more smoothly if the kids respect their parents, but we have other views on how the respect should be garnered. However, the goal remains the same: home preserving.

Perhaps the key is realizing that homes, like fruits and vegetables, need careful preserving, and that though the work is hard and fussy, the results are something to savour when the cold of winter settles in.

Perhaps the greatest social service that can be rendered by anybody to the country and to mankind is to bring up a family.

— George Bernard Shaw

Bless Your Bleeding Heart

Matthew 25:37–40

Then the righteous will answer him, "Lord, when was it that we saw you hungry and gave you food, or thirsty and gave you something to drink? And when was it that we saw you a stranger and welcomed you, or naked and gave you clothing? And when was it that we saw you sick or in prison and visited you?" And the king will answer them, "Truly I tell you, just as you did it to one of the least of these who are members of my family, you did it to me."

The other morning I was standing at the kitchen sink washing dishes, a country radio station playing softly in the background. When a song ended, the female announcer came on saying that the station had received varying response to their call-in poll regarding people's views on Roy Romanow's report on health care. Then she played some of the phone messages left by listeners, some in favour and some opposed to the changes Romanow proposed. One, in particular, stuck out.

"Nobody wants to hear it, but I'm going to say it anyway. We need to stop being such a bunch of bleeding hearts and quit giving all our money away to other countries."

This made my heart constrict a little and I said out loud to the suds, cereal bowl in hand, "Don't say that." She was right about one thing. I didn't want to hear it.

Now I want to say a bit about the theory of quantum physics. (Don't worry. I really am going somewhere with this.) You'll see I'm not a physicist. But I'm told that from the theory it follows that everything we say and we do continues to travel through space and time. Everything is connected, so our actions and words touch others and somehow alter the universe. We never function alone because each thing we do affects someone else in some way. According to the theory, in merely living we are connected to all creation.

Jesus puts it this way: "Whenever you did this for the least of these, you did it for me." When we provide shelter to the homeless, drink to the thirsty, and food to the hungry, we are doing it for Christ and for creation in its entirety — including ourselves. Make no mistake. Our actions, positive and negative, affect us as well as our neighbours. When we rape the land, we rape our children and grandchildren. When we build a hospital in Zambia, we apply balm to our own nation's wounds, and when we turn away from suffering half a world away, we condone suffering in our own homes.

Returning to the "bleeding heart" statement, what gives us the right to withhold what we have from others just because we are blessed to live where we live: blessed by an education, blessed with the right to vote, blessed by a relatively stable economy and rich resources? Surely we didn't plant the forests, put the fish in the sea, deposit the oil far beneath the rocks and soil. That's why they are blessings — because they're riches we've had no hand in producing. Sure, we have the brains to harvest them (ravenously), but so do the folks in Africa, given the same opportunity.

Nobody wants to hear it, but I'm going to say it anyway: These things do not belong to us.

It's possible that in having access to these treasures, we may *owe* something to the rest of the world, to Christ, to ourselves, to the future. That's a debt that can only be paid by sharing.

Love, tenderness, and compassion are real justice.
Justice without love is not justice.
Love without justice is not love.

— Mother Teresa

Not So Different
In God's Eyes

The Kingdom of God comes not at some future time
You cannot point out the sign of its coming
The Kingdom of God comes not at some special site
You cannot point out the place of its coming
The Kingdom of God is already here, among you, now

— from *The Essential Jesus* by John Dominic Crossan

few weeks ago I was driving alone to the church where I work. The wide urban streets were mostly deserted — rare, except at 7:30 on a Sunday morning. I remember enjoying the quiet and feeling happy as I descended a gentle paved hill to see that the traffic light at the bottom was green. But I couldn't turn immediately as there was a man in the crosswalk.

Before him he pushed a shopping cart heavy with bags, blankets, bottles, and a long smooth stick, perhaps a broom handle. He moved a little stiffly and I imagined he had just awakened from a less-than-deep sleep somewhere chilly, but there's no way I could know for sure. Lines etched his face and the thick white beard he sported must have provided some much needed protection from the elements, as did the rumpled canvas hat and winter coat he wore. He would have fitted behind the wheel of a Newfoundland fishing vessel better than on a downtown Alberta crosswalk. He had that weathered old-man-of-the-sea look about him.

As he moved close by my driver-side window our eyes locked, and then something happened that has stayed with me. At the same instant, we smiled — no, beamed — at one another for a long moment. He waved my way, lifting his hand just enough for me to see, and I nodded to acknowledge his gesture. Then we moved on and into our separate lives: me, the blond, church-workin' woman driving the little blue sports car, and he, a man who has seen more than I have and would spend the day trying to ensure he'd see the next one.

The experience meant something to me and I think to him also, but the significance was difficult to articulate until I happened to share the story with a group of colleagues. Someone said it best when she commented, "You recognized your shared humanity."

Yes! That's it exactly. We reached out in this big, bad world and saw each other for one blessed and holy moment the way God sees us. That's something worth sharing especially when we often feel so isolated from one another, feel like we're sprinting on parallel tracks that never intersect and wearing blinders that keep us unaware. It's when we recognize one another as beings created by and for God that we help to realize the Holy Spirit's kingdom on earth.

——

I am endeavouring to see God through service of humanity, for I know that God is neither in heaven nor down below, but in every one.

— Gandhi

About Thankfulness

Proverbs 3:6

In all your ways acknowledge him,
and he will make straight your paths.

I've been remembering my Grandma Knutson today, how I would spend weekends at her home in Hughenden where we'd visit over endless cups of thick coffee and games of Chinese checkers. She also loved yahtzee, and I knew enough not to mention the close link between it and poker, yahtzee's father. Who knows? Maybe she knew about yahtzee's family of origin, but if I'd brought it up, my grandma, on principle alone, would have refused to play and we'd have been cheated out of hours of fun.

On some afternoons, we'd drive to Wainwright where we'd eat at the café on main street and shop at Morgan's Family Department Store. During the journey there and back, just over half-an-hour's drive, we'd count the deer we spotted in the ditches and fields. Then we'd have cookies (that she'd baked, of course) and milk and go to bed.

In the morning over our empty cereal bowls and dainty cups and saucers, Grandma and I would bow our heads, and she would pray, "Heavenly Father, thank you for a good night's rest and for last night's rain. Thank you for good health, for the flowers that just came up in the garden, for the new birds at the feeder, and for this morning's sunshine. Thank you for a good visit with Lori and may she have a safe journey home. Amen."

What a great way to start the day. Yet I never prayed thanks when I wasn't at Grandma's — not growing up and not as an adult. Talk about self-denial!

Today, a gratitude journal is thought to be a helpful tool for improving one's outlook. It is suggested that when you get up in the morning you should list all the things you are thankful for in this book. It gives morale a boost and gets the mind focused on the good stuff in life. It's a simple activity that fosters a positive attitude.

Just like Grandma's breakfast grace.

She had a lot of good habits. My grandma would get up in the morning, and have a warm bath, and do her hair. When the weather permitted, she laid her deck table with fine china and silverware and ate in the shade of the full boughs of the weeping willow tree. She tended blooming house plants, kept the bird feeder and bird bath full, and was a regular correspondent with old friends. It's my perception that my grandmother lived her life with a keen awareness of the gifts she been given — a rich way to live.

Maybe the habit of her morning prayer of thankfulness accounted for the positive attitude that allowed her to make the most out of her simple life. She could just as easily have seen her life in rural Alberta as lonely and dull. After his final stroke that landed him for several years in an out-of-town nursing home, Grandpa died. Over the years following, so did many of her friends. As time moved on, the windows in the downtown shops were covered over one by one with brown paper, all three of the lumber yards closed, and they took down the old green water tower and boarded up two of the service stations.

But to the end Grandma looked at the good things she had, buoyed up perhaps by those morning prayers. As her former world died around her, her spirit was thankful for God's gifts and survived.

If the only prayer you said in your whole life was "thank you," that would suffice.

— Meister Eckhart

A Meeting Of Tiny Minds

Psalm 119:144

Give me understanding that I may live.

———

*Y*esterday I witnessed an amusing encounter between two of God's creatures. I was at my computer in what I call my writing corner. The writing corner features a computer desk, the shelf along its top laden with reference texts, on its surface, a telephone, stapler, paper pads, and a jar of pens and pencils, all within easy reach of the person (mostly me) working at the computer. The corner is at the far wall of the kitchen with a clear view of the bird feeder through the glass patio doors. It's a good place to work — close to the cookies and the tea kettle.

Otis, my black and white cat, enjoys the view of the bird feeder even more than I do. She sits for hours, staring at the flitting sparrows and chickadees, her tail flicking from side to side as she imagines that door suddenly sliding open, allowing her to pounce with a grace and stealth she doesn't possess in reality. For a strictly indoor cat the dream is a sweet one.

Then yesterday morning as she kept her vigil at the glass doors, a new figure emerged from the bushy depths of the large spruce tree directly in front of our balcony. He hopped limberly from a thick branch onto the wide wooden rail and sat there for a moment on his haunches, fluffing his great, grey tail and scoping the yard for food. When he spied the corn and sunflower seeds dropped and discarded by the songbirds, his black eyes sparkled.

For a while the squirrel ate completely unaware of the small, quivering form on the other side of the glass only about two feet away. Finally, a neat pile of sunflower seed shells at his feet, he looked up and around for more. He moved toward the glass in search of seeds. At the same time and from the inside, Otis also stepped toward the window, cautious but compelled by her curiosity.

The squirrel spotted Otis and their eyes locked. With only the glass separating them, they stared, two small brains struggling to evaluate the situation, to understand what was on the other side of the window. Finally, Otis lifted a careful white paw and placed it on the glass. At this gesture, the squirrel's ears perked forward in interest and he moved a tad closer, nose nearly touching the patio door. The two animals studied each other for a few moments with a greater intensity than I had assumed they were capable of. Then, very slowly, the squirrel took a couple of steps backwards before turning his plume of a tail and fleeing, first into the spruce and then into the street beyond, apparently returning home after his bold adventure to the other side of the road.

It seemed to me that Otis and the squirrel, for a period in time, really tried to see one another, viewed each other with the keenest kind of interest. I smiled because it was cute, but it also made me think seriously (as everything does!) about how God would have us see one another. How often we go through life not noticing the other beings created equally in God's love. How much we have to share with each other that we withhold. I wonder what I could learn from just one other person if I viewed him or her with the wonder and intensity with which those two furry beings saw each other.

Of course, it would make any sane person really nervous if I stared at them as unbrokenly as the cat and squirrel stared. But couldn't I show the same kind of interest and try to see people as God sees them? The experience would make my daily interactions into something wonderful. And, in the process, I might be seeing God's creatures as they were intended by the Creator to be seen.

If we have no peace, it is because we have forgotten that we belong to each other.

— Mother Teresa

Accept Your Neighbour

Mark 12:28–31

One of the scribes came near and heard them disputing
with one another, and seeing that he answered them well,
he asked him, "Which commandment is the first of all?"
Jesus answered, "The first is, 'Hear, O Israel: the Lord our
God, the Lord is one; so you shall love the Lord your God
with all your heart, and with all your soul, and with all
your mind, and with all your strength.' The second is this,
'You shall love your neighbour as yourself.' There is no
other commandment greater than these."

———

*Y*ou can't get along with everyone. Fact is, we're all so different, so
uniquely created, that there'll usually be someone who just rubs
us the wrong way in whatever situation we may find ourselves. A
person who talks too much or someone who talks too little; a gossip,
a nag, a braggart, a skinflint, a stickler for detail; or one of those
people who just slaps everything together. Or maybe someone whose
thinking differs drastically from ours, or — worse yet — someone
whose way of perceiving the world is so much like ours that they
drive us crazy with it. Most likely the person we have most diffi-
culty with will be someone who reminds in some very strong way
of ourselves.

I think it's safe to say that most of us don't always get along with
ourselves. I know I'm often plagued with self-doubt and disappointments regarding what I have or haven't accomplished. Much time is
spent in the private space of my head, criticizing and judging myself,
wondering if I'm really up to this job of life at all, and then worrying
that perhaps others will notice that I'm not up to it. Then what?

It seems most of us are tormented by inner conflict, by unrealis-
tic expectations of ourselves, and maybe by a lack of self-discipline
placing us in situations where we let ourselves down.

"Love your neighbour as yourself." So what does God expect of us according to this commandment? That we love everyone all the time? That we never become annoyed or that we never withdraw? That we laugh at every obnoxious joke shared by every socially-maladjusted loudmouth between here and Mexico City? That we put our hearts on the line for the faultiest of lovers and offer our trust to the most disloyal of friends? I doubt this is the point. We are after all human, and it is God who made us so. And as a car manufacturer is fully aware of the potential of the vehicle, our Creator is also aware of what we are capable.

The way I see it is that we can only love others the way we love (or don't love) ourselves. Herein lies the most important reason for self-acceptance. If we can't accept, love, or understand ourselves, we won't be able to extend these feelings to anyone else. Love and acceptance doesn't mean we need to hang out with the people who drive us berserk. It simply allows us to relate better to people we don't always understand and to accept that everyone comes from a different place and brings a different gift to the party.

The two commandments fit together: loving God and loving ourselves. In loving God, we may learn to love, understand, and accept ourselves. That's why that commandment comes first perhaps. Then, in loving God we are able to extend love to our neighbours as we give it to ourselves.

People take different roads seeking fulfillment and happiness. Just because they're not on your road doesn't mean they've gotten lost.

— H. Jackson Brown, Jr.

Be Generous With
Your Band-Aids

Mark 1:40–41

A leper came to him begging him, and kneeling he said to
him, "If you choose, you can make me clean." Moved with
pity, Jesus stretched out his hand and touched him, and said,
"I do choose. Be made clean!"

———

*W*hile getting dressed that evening I reached into my vest pocket
because I thought I had heard some soft crinkling against the
pocket's lining. There my hand touched a couple narrow paper pack-
ages joined by a perforated line. Band-Aids! I was particularly surprised
to find them because for the preceding week or so the average age of
my students had been twenty-three years old — an age group rarely
requiring Band-Aids.

Then I remembered the Friday I had last worn the vest. It was
one of those days that I'd been asked to teach Grade 1. This early in
the year, many of the little ones find the long days really long and the
attention to be slim pickin's compared to what they receive at home.
(One student asked me that same day around 10:30 in the morning
if it was almost home time. "I wish, honey. I wish.") So as I pass their
tiny desks, they often extend their hands, palms up or fingers extended, and say, "Look, Teacher," and with very grave, concerned
expressions put on, they show me a variety of minor cuts, scrapes,
and hangnails.

I found I was expending far too much time and energy dashing
back and forth to the teacher's desk to fetch Band-Aids. Yet the apparent healing property inherent in those adhesive strips borders on
the miraculous — and so I stuffed several of these sticky reassurances
into my pocket to save myself two hundred steps. This solution made
the healing much more convenient.

Of course, I didn't have an obligation to give a Band-Aid to each child who thought he was in need of some comfort, but once that comfort was in my pocket, it really wasn't a problem to give it. This turned out to be a very efficient way of keeping the kids satisfied and yet allowing me to actually teach them something on a Friday in September. By noon, nearly everyone was wearing a Band-Aid.

As we get older, we learn how to handle our long, long days and how to hide our hurts. We may crave reassurances and comfort, but we don't seek either as openly as do small children. That's why, as adults, we must be much more in tune with each other to know when someone really does need a kind word, a hug, a pat on the back — if we choose to care, that is.

And make no mistake. The decision to give the comfort we can or to withhold it is solely up to us. In Mark 1, the leper tells Jesus, "If you choose, you can make me clean." And Jesus does choose. I don't believe that choice is an accidental detail included in this story. I think it's there to illustrate our potential to do good deeds if we will or desire to.

Sometimes we convince ourselves that we are in no position to give the emotional support someone else is thirsty for. Maybe it is inconvenient for us. But an inconvenience is very different from an impossibility. If it's a priority for us to love our neighbours, we will create ways to make showing that love convenient. I picture us all moving through the world wishing it were home time at 10:30 in the morning, our pockets filled with colourful, comforting Band-Aids. We never stop to count the number we give and nor do we ever run out. It's as if the Band-Aids replenish themselves as rapidly as we freely distribute them.

It's a habit I'm going to continue. Whenever I teach young children, I'll always keep the Band-Aids within easy grasp, for it's just as easy to comfort a wound than to overlook it. So with adults. I only need to be better prepared for the circumstance when it arises. There's nothing impossible about it.

Bound By Fishy Threads

Deuteronomy 34:4–6

The Lord said to him, "This is the land of which I swore to
Abraham, to Isaac, and to Jacob, saying, 'I will give it to
your descendants'; I have let you see it with your eyes, but
you shall not cross over there." Then Moses, the servant of
the Lord, died there in the land of Moab, at the Lord's
command. He was buried in a valley in the land
of Moab, opposite Beth-peor, but no one knows his
burial place to this day.

———

*W*e arrived at the country hall and, pulling into the parking lot,
were surprised by how crowded it was on that Sunday evening.
The stars were just beginning to poke out of their darkening blue
backdrop as we got out of the car and made our way toward the front
steps. It was there that it hit us.

"Ugh! What's that smell? That's not *it*, is it?" I had warned my
companion earlier about what he might face that evening at dinner
and he was already a little edgy. I was happy to confirm his fears.

"Yup. That's it. That's the stuff. That's lutefisk!"

For some of you, an introduction to this traditional Norwegian
delicacy may be necessary, although its reputation, like its smell, often precedes it. Lutefisk is fish, usually cod, soaked in lye where it
rots and becomes like jelly. When this point of perfection has been
reached, it is thoroughly rinsed. And then the gelatinous mass is
heated, doused with melted butter, and eaten lustily.

Why do we eat it? (Well, actually I don't. I can't. I've tried. Several times.) The reason is simple enough. We eat it because those
who came before us ate it, and those who came before them, and those
who came yet before them. Like it or not, it's a part of who we are, a
smelly piece of what ties us by its fishy threads to history.

Over four years ago, my Grandma Knutson died. It was she who did all the traditional cooking and who took me to my first lutefisk supper. Now that she's gone, I feel strongly compelled to find out more about where I've come from and to maintain many of the traditions into which she breathed life. That's what must have brought me to the lutefisk supper that Sunday night, because it most certainly wasn't the promise of the jiggly fish that lured me.

I had a craving to be in a room full of people who shared my past, who talked about the things my grandparents used to. I didn't know most of those people in attendance. Our present lives never brushed shoulders, but our pasts collided and embraced continuously. I wanted to be there, where I would be recognized, not as a teacher or a writer or a church member, but as a Son of Knut. With that common bond guiding me, it was easy to step into a hall packed with strangers. Because of where my great-great-great grandparents hailed from, I fitted right in.

I was the opposite of Moses, yet somewhat the same. While Moses died with a glimpse of his homeland lying just beyond his reach, I was born with my homeland showing only in the rearview mirror. Yet Moses and I share the same yearning for what we know is there, where we know we belong. It's very possible that I will not ever see my "homeland" either.

But that's all right. I just need to know that it's there. At lutefisk suppers, while others devour fish, I'll fill up on traditional Norwegian desserts and on every word of every story, devouring the details like an orphan listening to stories of lost parents. Unlike Moses' followers, I can't know where I'm going but I'll do what I can to figure out where I've come from. Who knows? In doing so, I may also discover my destination and without a doubt I'll find a bit of myself as well. Thank goodness this journey of discovery isn't dependent in any way upon having to swallow even one rounded forkful of lutefisk!

Love is touching souls.

— Joni Mitchell

A Dog's Good Taste

Psalm 139:1–3

O Lord, you have searched me
and known me.
You know when I sit down and
when I rise up;
you discern my thoughts from
far away.
You search out my path and my
lying down,
and are acquainted with all
my ways.

---

*S*ometime in October the phone call came.

"Lori, I found your Christmas present today! It's the funniest thing — I can't believe I found it!"

"Gimme a hint — but just one. I don't want to guess."

"Oh, I'll give you as many hints as you want. Don't worry. You'll never guess in a million years! Okay, here's a hint: you're the only person I know who will even know what this is, let alone what to do with it."

"Big or small?"

"Big for its kind."

"Old or new?"

"Definitely old."

And so the questions and answers continued to pass between us during the weeks leading up to Christmas until finally the day arrived and my curiosity was satisfied.

In the exhaust-clouded parking lot on that minus-twenty-seven-degrees-afternoon, she pulled the mystery gift from the trunk of the car. She'd been right. I would never have guessed in a million years what she had found for me in the dust and dim of an out-of-town thrift store. Laughing, she handed it to me and half- apologized, "I got it for 75 cents because a dog tried to eat it."

Sure enough. Two thick corners had been gnawed off that single ten pound volume of Strong's *Exhaustive Concordance of the Bible*, complete with Greek and Hebrew dictionaries but, miraculously, none of the print had been chewed or drooled away. It was mine! All mine!

I couldn't believe my luck! Why had this tooth-marked treasure landed in my lap? Really, that's the important part: how had it found its way to me? The answer, of course is through my friend. But my friend would never have known to pick up that great hulk of a book full of Biblical technicalities in print so small you'd need a microscope to read the italic print if she hadn't known all about me.

So! She was really and truly listening last year when I was taking that Hebrew scriptures course and making awkward use of Strong's *Concordance* on-line. None of that "in one ear, out the other" stuff for her. Nope. She had filed it away under "Useful Information Regarding Who Lori Is" for future reference.

Realizing how well my friend knew me made me feel loved and cared about. The details of my life just aren't that exciting, but she took those tiny, dry details I tossed to her and caught them in midair before they lost their motion, storing them away, fragile and light as potpourri, to consider later.

The book was a great gift but the greatest gift is the realization that someone knows us, that we are understood and accepted despite our idiosyncrasies. The best confirmation that we are not alone is simply being known.

And in finding, buying and presenting me with that monstrous book that she had to store somewhere for all those weeks and then lug into town, my friend showed me that she knew me. For sure, that's evidence that she loves me, and that's a Christmas gift even richer than the book is heavy.

No man is so poor as to have nothing worth giving. Give what you have. To someone it may be better than you dare to think.

— Henry Wadsworth Longfellow

Broader Views

I Love Alberta Beef
(And Jesus, Too)

Mark 7:6–7

He said to them, "Isaiah prophesied rightly about you hypocrites, as it is written, 'This people honours me with their lips, but their hearts are far from me; in vain do they worship me, Teaching human precepts as doctrines.' "

---

*T*he other day I was driving along a busy thoroughfare but holding my own. In my haste in the centre lane, I caught up to an older white pick-up truck. On its scrubbed-clean rear bumper were two stickers. The one on the left read "I Love Jesus," with the word "Love" indicated by a Valentine heart. The sticker on the right, bearing the same red heart along with the blacked-in shaped of our own dear province, said proudly, "I Love Alberta Beef."

I laughed out loud. Now the challenge lies with me to explain exactly why these two bumper-sharing stickers brought me sudden mirth — and a challenge it will be because I'm not entirely certain myself.

On the surface, I suppose, it was funny simply because the stickers looked so similar. Both white and rectangular, the same size with the same bold, black print and Valentine hearts, yet expressing two completely disparate ideas. One clearly expresses an economic support of the beef production industry in Alberta while the other very publicly identifies the vehicle owner (I presume) as a Christian. Both stickers claim to love something in the same manner but surely, if asked, the driver would acknowledge that the two have only the manger in common, one eating from it, the other lying in it. That's where the comparison ends.

Ahh-haa! This could be it. I think I laughed because I wondered in that moment what Jesus would think of the juxtaposed statements of adoration. Don't think here that I am claiming to know the mind of Jesus —— these are just the ramblings and musings of my imagination. Having said that ....

Picture the Saviour returned and choosing a largish city in one of the richest places on earth to begin his task. He's cruising down one of the city's major arteries in his beat-up 1974 Toyota Tercel, fuzzy dice swinging with the ups and downs of the road, the dial tuned in to talk radio. Jesus is travelling to his volunteer job at an inner-city shelter and drug rehab facility when he spots the bumper stickers nearly level with his line of sight.

How does he react? But this isn't the first time it's happened. He sees indications of his worship on cars and vans all over the highways and biways. Little Jesus fish, the same simple shape his followers drew in the dust to identify themselves while avoiding persecution following his crucifixion, now boldly adorn the rear doors of mini-vans. On other vehicles he's seen chapter and verse displayed more times than he can count: John 3:16. On still others a gazillion bumper stickers of varying size, shape, and colour proclaim love for him. And now he and Alberta beef share the same Valentine heart.

I can't imagine it any other way. I envision him laughing with wonder at his name shown in such a sincere, silly way, stuck to automobiles that cost more than the homes inhabited by most of the world's population, automobiles heavily dependent upon oil, the greed for which inspires conflict and war.

He shakes his head and laughs. What else could he do?

———

We call it a Society; and go about professing openly
the totalest separation, isolation. Our life is not a
mutual helpfulness; but rather, cloaked under due
laws-of-war, named "fair competition" and so forth,
it is a mutual hostility.

— Thomas Carlyle

Voices

Psalm 19:1–4

The heavens are telling the glory
of God;
and the firmament proclaims
his handiwork.
Day to day pours forth speech,
and night to night declares
knowledge.
There is no speech, nor are there
words;
their voice is not heard;
yet their voice goes out through
all the earth,
and their words to the end of
the world.

It's been a summer of typical Alberta weather in that a few electrical storms have been mixed in with everything else. During one of these, when lightning flashed across a darkened sky and the voice of thunder shook the window panes and tingled the soles of our feet, the power at my friends' house went out.

"It was so quiet," my friend told me. "We talked and talked, and then Sheldon took a nap and I did some reading."

She continued her reflections. There are so many noises in a house produced by the constant, unseen presence of electricity that we grow to accept them until they go unnoticed — until they are suddenly absent. The reassuring hum of the fridge, the tick of Grandpa's grandfather clock, the twang of the kitchen radio interspersed with static and weather reports — all fill the air around us, wrapping us in everyday comfort. We take electricity, its comforts, and the sounds it produces for granted — until they're gone. Since they don't normally let us down, we seldom acknowledge their presence.

My friend explained how the silence reminded her of God —
how it seemed to her that God's voice was finally allowed to come
through when the clutter of electrical noise stopped. The silence
brought her and her husband the opportunity for some quiet time in
which to share their thoughts and then spend some time together in
silence as only people very comfortable with one another can do.

I liked her take on it, but my view was different.

"Good point," I replied, "but I perceive God as being like those
ever-present sounds that fill the day and night, surrounding us, touching us with the gentle ticking of the clock or bathing us in the gentle,
reassuring hum from the refrigerator."

Well, maybe I wasn't quite that poetic at the time, but this is my
piece and I can make myself out to be Shakespeare if I want.

Often we may feel that God is absent because we don't notice the
presence, but I argue that we've never known what it's like to be
completely without God. It's a power that doesn't go out.

It's interesting that both my friend and I could put very different
spins on the same event and still come out having insight to share
into what God's presence means for us. It's great to know that whether
the electricity fails or remains true, neither of us will be in the dark
about how we think about the Creator.

People see God every day;
they just don't recognize Him.

— Pearl Bailey

Chase the Money Changers
From the Temple

Matthew 21:12–14

Then Jesus entered the temple and drove out all who were
selling and buying in the temple, and he overturned the
tables of the money changers
and seats of those who sold doves. He said to them, "It is
written,
'My house shall be called a house of prayer';
but you are making it a den of robbers."
The blind and the lame came to him in the temple, and he
cured them.

———

I was watching an episode of *The Dini Petty Show* the other day.
She had as her guest an extraordinary woman very different from
the polished and smiling TV people we're used to seeing on the talk
show set. The woman had formerly been a Roman Catholic nun
who began her career doing mission work overseas. Her job was to
care for the poor, the weak, and the dying, and doing so changed her
outlook forever.

A hard life had given her a hard, serious edge. She spoke of the
hardship, death, and poverty she witnessed close-up every day. She
experienced firsthand how apathy in the Western world stunts and
threatens social and economic progress in poorer countries. She gave
no flashing white smile to remember her by, but the words she spoke
in her flat tone regarding our inaction have stuck with me all week:
"Stop buying your stuff, and look at what's going on all around you!"

You see, she has been there and has seen that apathy is not without consequences. On the contrary, our inaction can be devastating.
And this apathy amid all our wealth and all our political clout frus-
trates her.

I thought about it. What keeps me from acting? I can write. So what stops me from just writing one letter a month on behalf of Amnesty International? I have the time to do this. No problem. But I don't. I don't because I am afraid. I am scared to become as aware as this strong woman who surrounded herself with the world's suffering. What if I thought about it too much, and unlike that tough woman, I was crushed by sorrow and my own feelings of helplessness?

These thoughts caused me to look again at Jesus' act of chasing the money changers from the temple. Upon looking again at this story from Matthew I noticed for the first time what Jesus does after cleansing the temple: he goes on to cure the blind and the lame. He takes action. He realized that people had suffered and died in poverty and loneliness for generations before his birth and would continue to suffer for generations following his death. At times he must have felt overwhelmed by it all. Still, he did what he could to change the injustices and the pain he saw.

There is a place and a time for "buying stuff." Sometimes it's necessary stuff and sometimes it's just fun stuff. I think it's okay to have fun shopping. But the former nun on *The Dini Petty Show* was reminding us that we in North America have let consumerism, the act of buying stuff, become our focus, so we don't focus on real problems which, if we pull together, we have the power and resources to alleviate.

Wow. No wonder she's frustrated. She's up against something huge: our apathy. And beneath our apathy lies fear — a fear that keeps us buying stuff and preventing us from looking beyond our own borders except for perhaps a tropical vacation.

But as the passage from Matthew showed me, there is room for everything: shopping, reflection, and generous action. Perhaps we first need to clear a space in our lives where stuff isn't allowed in. Then in that place, we can pray for courage to overcome the apathy that prevents us from taking those first small steps in the direction of change.

—

It is preoccupation with possessions, more than anything else, that prevents men from living freely and nobly.

— Bertrand Russell

Who Loves Humanity?

John 15:18–20

If the world hates you, be aware that it hated me
before it hated you. If you belonged to the world, the world
would love you as its own. Because you do not belong to
the world, but I have chosen you out of the world —
therefore the world hates you. Remember the word I said to
you, "Servants are not greater than their master." If they
persecuted me, they will persecute you; if they kept my
word, they will keep yours also.

---

*R*ecently I attended a folk music festival in northern Alberta,
and performing there was an extraordinary African musician who
reminded us all, as we stood drenched and cold before the main stage,
that rain is a blessing. He spoke both of the greatness of nature and
also about things he couldn't comprehend. One of these was the horrific massacre that took place not so long ago in Rwanda. He was
shocked and grief-stricken over the senseless genocide, but even more
by the fact that the world watched it all happen and let it continue.

I shared his sadness and bewilderment at how we can view the
slaughtering of one million people with less emotion than we watch
Who Wants To Be A Millionaire. We empathize with the people on the
"hot seat" and want so badly for them to win. When they do, we
rejoice; when they don't, we feel disappointed. Where is that heart-
felt involvement when the TV screen presents images of slain men,
women, and children? Are we more interested in someone becoming
instantly wealthy for no substantial reason than in someone being
instantly decapitated or tortured to death?

Up on the main stage, the musician cried out to the crowd, "Who
here loves humanity? Who has faith in humanity?" Everyone present
cheered and bounced up and down. He repeated the questions, louder
this time, and again the crowd shouted louder and leapt higher.

I didn't understand how the African artist got from speaking of the horrendous crimes we commit against each other's bodies and souls to encouraging the crowd to profess their love for and faith in humanity. After considering it for a while, I came to the conclusion that what he wanted from the people gathered there was an assurance that they themselves would not condone or accept crimes against humanity and that they would not commit or encourage these types of crimes.

But I was left standing among the dancing revellers feeling numb and distant. I felt this way because I'm not sure I can manage to love and have faith in humanity.

It hurts me that there is so much pain, death, and injustice in the world. And I think maybe the victims are the members of humanity the musician wanted us to love. But I get stuck on the unavoidable fact that it was another part of humanity who inflicted hatred upon this less powerful, arguably gentler part. The murderers as well as the victims are human. I find that I'm unable to love or have faith in all of humanity. I'd be boldly lying if I leapt up and shouted with the rest of the crowd because, when I think about all the faces of humanity and all its contradictions, I just can't. When we're good, we're a fairly nice lot, but when we're bad, we're evil.

That's why I seek faith in the divine. I don't believe it's in our human nature to do really great, loving things. It's in our nature to survive, compete, and to look out for ourselves. I would argue that it's something divine both within us and outside us that impels us to move beyond our human nature. Divinity inspires art, generosity, and self-sacrifice. Humanity itself just isn't enough to put all my faith in. It's guaranteed to let me down again and again.

Our membership in humanity allows us to walk the face of the earth and to sample the wonderful things life has to offer but it's that divine spark within that can inspire us to be a little more than human. Now that's something to have faith in.

Our humanity is a poor thing, except for the divinity that
stirs within us.

— Francis Bacon

The World Uncoloured
By Stained Glass

Matthew 6:20

But lay up for yourselves treasures in heaven, where neither
moth nor rust corrupts, and where thieves do not break
through nor steal.

My life is bombarded by shards of media coming at me through
the television, Internet, newspapers, and the radio. So it's not
often that I feel fortunate in stumbling over a piece of news. But this
was different, a story I never dreamed I'd find. It lifted my heart and
at the same time pushed me way beyond my comfort level.

On page 3 of *The Independent on Sunday*, a British newspaper,
the headline read, "Church sells its silver to feed the poor." Of course,
I read on. As it turns out, Holy Trinity Church in Edinburgh, Scotland, plans to sell its seventeenth-century, eighteen-piece silver
communion set to the National Museum of Scotland for £200,000
in order to feed the poor residents of impoverished Wester Hailes, at
whose heart the old church stands.

The Lewes Road United Reformed Church in Brighton demol-
ished their original church building and re-established a worship
location a short distance away. On the site of the former church,
congregation members designed a new building that would house a
local doctor's office on the ground floor where, at that busy central
location, it would be very accessible to the elderly. St. John's United
Reformed Church in Ipswich also created a new, more active role for
itself in its community when it replaced its church and gardens with
low-income housing for elderly people. On the new site, they erected
a smaller building for worship and also for the use of local day groups.

Holy Trinity Church in Wester Hailes already runs a breakfast
club for school children, an emergency food store for desperate families,

a free clothing store, a drop-in centre for teenagers and provides counsel-
ling services to drug addicts. Wow. Feeding and clothing the poor, caring
for those set aside and avoided by mainstream society. Reminds me of
the ministry led and encouraged by a certain man from Galilee.

It is challenging: what to do with our emptying church buildings as worship attendance continues to rapidly decrease. We become
frantic to fill them, to bring people back to God's house for a visit.
The change is frightening, but need we be afraid? Is it possible that
this is meant to be more exciting than fear-provoking? Could it be
that God's house is undergoing an inestimable expansion and blessed
renovations? Is there a chance that the Spirit is pushing down these
walls and moving out into the streets to embrace those at the curbside?

I think the reason I found this article so uplifting is that it sounds
not like death but like resurrection. In this time of popularity of New
Age and individualistic thinking an increasingly socially responsible
church gives me hope for the world.

Don't get me wrong. The loss of our churches is a tragedy that I
would greatly mourn. My own history is bound tightly to those grand
structures reaching skyward and smelling comfortably of polished
wood and pressed pages. We need not lose our church buildings, but
for the church to live and sustain others, the functions of these monu-
ments must change and expand. As time moves onward, the troubled
planet and its people call to the followers of Jesus, urging us to step
outside those heavy wooden doors, to see the world clearly and
uncoloured by stained glass.

Jesus never said that he would be easy to follow. Or that it would
be particularly comfortable. Or that God's kingdom had in mind
our maximum earning potential. The answer, if we want it, lies right
before us. It's not a mystery, a puzzle to be solved, or a secret to hear.
It's only a difficult thing for us to do.

———

Anything you cannot relinquish when it has outlived its
usefulness possesses you, and in this materialistic age a great
many of us are possessed by our possessions.

— Peace pilgrim

Green Hair and Atomic Orange Juice

2 Corinthians 4:16–18

So we do not lose heart. Even though our outer nature is wasting away, our inner nature is being renewed day by day. For this slight momentary affliction is preparing us for an eternal weight of glory beyond all measure, because we look not at what can be seen but at what cannot be seen; for what can be seen is temporary, but what cannot be seen is eternal.

—•—

I've gotten used to the green and orange images filling my television screen, and I can depend on my active imagination to work overtime while I'm viewing to fill in all the missing colour variations. The only objects on screen that look right are Kermit the Frog, the Green Giant, and the luscious fruit displayed in orange juice commercials. (Not the juice itself — it's kind of an atomic vermilion, more like antifreeze than a breakfast beverage.)

Not everyone would feel this way, but for me the absence of a working TV remote control device in the house has been beneficial. You see, I used to have a problem with channel-surfing. Well, no longer! It's surprising what you'll find interesting as long as your other option is getting off the couch and turning the channel. I once watched a screen displaying the words: "Trouble is temporary. Please do not adjust your set." So I didn't and sure enough, the trouble was temporary. After thirty-five minutes, the screen flashed on part way through a sitcom and I felt triumphant in not having gotten off the couch but choosing to wait it out.

Another thing that others may find bothersome is the shortage of "hook-ups" for cable, VCRs, and video games on the big dusty back of the TV. There is only one of these little dealies on my set. I've noticed recently that the new-fangled TVs have two, three, or more. People are just getting greedy or lazy or both. One dealy works fine. It just requires, once again, a little additional movement on the viewer's (that's me) part.

Whenever I want to watch a video, I simply lug my TV (which weighs about ten more pounds than I do) out from the wall, get down on my knees — not to pray, although it wouldn't hurt, but to switch around cords. I take out the cord running from the cable outlet in the wall out of the dealy in back of my TV and replace it with the one running from the VCR. No big deal if it's what you're used to.

I think a friend of mine said it best when she brought over a movie to watch at my place one evening: "Lori, your TV sucks." I could only agree. But it's how I've gotten used to seeing the TV world and it doesn't bother me as much as putting out the cash for a new one.

We all see things differently. To my friend, abreast of all the new TV technological advances since 1974, my TV sucks. But I wouldn't know. I see my TV the way I see it just as I see the world the way I see it: differently than everyone else. Yet we can still discuss what was on last night and I'll know what she's talking about. I'm up on current events. I wonder why the anchor has pale green hair receding from his orange-tinted forehead. But I understand the tragedies he brings into my living room.

It's a gift to perceive the world in different ways and to share with one another our varying perceptions. It's through these perceptions that we can expand each other's window on the world and on God's creation. Perhaps it's because we can't help but have a narrow view of life that each of us has a different one. That way, we all have something to give as well as a chance to widen our own views and, if we're lucky, maybe a chance to show one another shadows of a faith that can't be seen, only felt and shared.

—-—

Life ... it tends to respond to our outlook, to shape
itself to meet our expectations.

— Richard M. DeVos

Life Happens

The Ghost Of
Fridge-Cleaning Past

Nehemiah 6:11

But I said, "Should a man like me run away?"

I stepped out onto the balcony and breathed in the sweet autumn night air, leaning over the railing in the privacy that darkness provides, and savouring it all for a couple of moments. In that pleasant place I thought, "Why don't I take advantage of this little retreat space right outside my patio doors more often?"

When I turned around to go back in, I received an answer to my silent musing. There it lay, shoved up against that tiny section of wall between the balcony's floor and the base of the sliding doors like the terrifying Ghost of Fridge-Cleaning Past to remind me eternally of the things I've put off.

How long had the Tupperware container full of rotten cauliflower been there, I couldn't remember. But I could remember how it got onto the balcony:

"Ugh! What's that smell?"

"I dunno. You take the garbage out?"

"Yeah. Of course I did."

"Hmm. Maybe it's coming from the fridge."

So I bravely pulled open the door and my friend and I stood back as the interior light illuminated several suspects. It was like a police line-up in which anyone could be guilty. I was certain we had identified the offender correctly when the thawed-for-a-few-days minute steak took that last long walk out to the dumpster. But the next day, the offensive smell remained and, as sometimes happens, the innocent had been wrongly convicted.

Then one evening while preparing lunch for the following work day, I remembered the head of cauliflower I had chopped up and stored in the clear container with the blue lid intending to stock my lunches with it. I slid it from the shelf and pried off the lid.

When I regained consciousness, I hadn't the strength or courage to carry the vile mess to the dumpster, so I banished it to the balcony, promising it and myself that I would deal with the problem tomorrow.

Isn't that just what we do with some of the biggest messes in our lives? Those lingering odours, that unsightly mould? With our strained relationships, unpaid credit card bills, our unfinished business? Afraid to deal with them or not knowing how, we leave them until they become something really difficult to handle.

Uneasy relationships and old grudges, set out on the balcony of our minds and hearts, fester and rot. They don't disappear; they even have a nasty tendency of appearing in our dreams and cropping up in our imaginations with increased frequency. Sometimes wouldn't just dealing with this garbage be a whole lot easier than harbouring it? Probably, but the challenge is pretty daunting. Often we don't even know where to begin.

For me, a good place to start is prayer. The only thing that makes me feel I'm not alone in the messes I've made is asking for God's presence and for the courage to do what is no longer avoidable. God is always there — I can count on that. The rest is up to me. But knowing that I'm not alone in facing my mistakes, my immoralities, the small disasters resulting from my humanness gives me the strength I need to take action. Sometimes. Other times, a lot more prayer and mental preparation is required before I can act.

So, as soon as I'm done this article, I'll slip on a pair of yellow rubber gloves, slide open those patio doors and whisper one final prayer as I finally deal with what should have been done long ago. True, facing the issue will be smelly business, but knowing it's done will feel terrific!

———

Be a strong little marshmallow.

— seen on a bumper sticker

I Got Myself Into this Jam

Haggai 1:9

You have looked for much, and, lo, it came to little;
and when you brought it home, I blew it away.

---

*S*tanding in my tiny kitchen, I hold my breath, pick up a jar of the saskatoon jelly that I made just twenty-six hours ago and gradually tip it to see if it's set. To my dismay, the dark purple concoction in the 250-ml jar sloshes up against the glass as easily as water. The answer to my question.

Ever the optimist, I leave the jars sitting overnight one more time. In the morning I sneak up on them as a seasoned hunter would deer grazing in an open meadow, gently snatch the closest jar from the herd and tip it gently to one side. Then I mutter some undeserved obscenity about jams and jellies in general.

What bothers me the most about this whole exploit is that I think I know what the problem is, and it is completely and easily avoidable. The explanation lies in the type of fruit pectin that I've used. For some reason unknown to me, I have never had any luck with powdered pectin. My jams and jellies end up as syrup each time I use it. (I refuse to put a flowery label on the jars boasting their contents as "Saskatoon Syrup" as if that's what I had intended to create all along.) Still, every once in a while I try it again, hoping and half expecting that it will work this time. It hasn't yet.

When I'm able to find it, I buy the liquid fruit pectin. It has successfully set my jams and jellies every time I've employed it so far. So why not use it every time? Am I merely a sucker for punishment or does the problem run a little deeper than that?

Someone once told me that repeatedly following the same course of action while expecting a different outcome each time is indicative of insanity. So what do my jelly-making experiences tell about me? I guess nothing I haven't suspected for a while now.

We all act crazy now and then, doing things that we know intuitively and from experience will land us in trouble. Yet, we're surprised when we land in trouble. We say, "Why does this always happen to me?" and "How come I have such bad luck?" Then we furrow our brows in an imitation of trying to understand when we know all along where the problem lies.

So often, experience tells us what to do and, more specifically, what *not* to do. Still we stubbornly pursue what we think is best for us, regardless of all the evidence presented to the contrary. Instead of looking at the facts (for example, powdered pectin doesn't work for me), we try to force things to turn out the way we think they should. This perseverance keeps us blind to the way things are.

My misguided trust in powdered pectin has led me from the path of successful jam and jelly production into failure. My own unwillingness to let go of old ideas has robbed me of a potentially richer and more satisfying experience. It is with this realization that I will enter the grocery stores of my future and only purchase products that, experience shows, give me the results I've sought.

And I will try to view my old, frustrating habits in the same way: not as comfortable old friends but as captors that keep me from the freedom of doing things differently. Who knows? Perhaps the jars upon jars of well-set preserves lining the pantry shelves won't outnumber the new blessings filling my life once I've made room for them and invited them in.

Do what you have always done and
you'll get what you have always got.

— Sue Knight

Two Small Guilts

Proverbs 20:9

Who can say, "I have made my heart clean;
I am pure from my sin"?

I finally got all my stuff moved from the dusty storage compartment into my new place, and over the course of a few long days I went through the process of rediscovering the things I'd packed into which boxes. I had tried to label most of the boxes accurately, but it still seemed like a treasure hunt. The two sets of shower curtain hooks still haven't turned up, and there's a critical shortage of tea towels in the kitchen, but everything else seems to be more or less accounted for.

While unpacking and organizing, I came upon something that made me really think and really feel. In my haste to get packed, the "q" I had printed on one of the boxes in thick blue marker had become a "g." The result was that the contents of that particular carton became "Two Small Guilts" instead of "Two Small Quilts." Something warm and comforting had been turned into something cold and discomforting.

God knows I wish there were only two! There are many more than that, and when they're weighing on my heart and mind, they sure don't feel small. The question is: What do we do with these guilts? Is it ever healthy and helpful to feel guilty for a time or is it a perfectly useless and destructive emotion that does nothing but eat steadily away at our energy stocks? Is guilt a road sign that I need to pause and pay attention to, or is it something to be ignored or avoided?

Before I began work on this article I searched the Bible for insight into what guilt is. From the information I was able to glean, it seems that the authors view guilt as the inevitable consequence of sin. Especially in the Old Testament, guilt is described as a sure judgement, a pronouncement of wrongdoing often on a whole people and their descendants, but and not as the uncomfortable individual emotion I'm addressing here.

I don't know if I came away with any answers, but I did leave my time of reflection wishing that my guilts over past mistakes and hurtful deeds could be as neatly folded and packed away as the two small quilts I had boxed-up and then stumbled upon again.

If for some reason we'd benefit from experiencing a little guilt, I wish that we could delve into an efficiently packed and labelled box of it, take out the contents, and examine them until we had learned their lesson. When we're done, it'd be grand if we could just tuck them back into place, tape the box tightly shut, and put it away. Then it wouldn't clutter up our lives and confuse our minds.

Guilt upon the conscience, like rust upon iron,
both defiles and consumes it, gnawing and creeping into
it, as that does which at last eats out the very heart and
substance of the metal.

—Bishop Robert South

Power To the Powerless

Proverbs 27:3

A stone is heavy, and sand is
weighty,
but a fool's provocation is
heavier than both.

I knelt at the front of the empty church sanctuary half an hour before the service was set to begin, not in devout prayer as you might imagine, but instead trying frantically to cram the microphone plug into its outlet.

It's hardly any secret that I am technologically inept. Because I believe this, whenever confronted with even the simplest of technological challenges — say, adjusting the toaster so that toast pops up light instead of dark brown — I become flustered, awkward, ready to launch into a rant.

Up there all by myself at the front of the church, I had already decided that, when I had finally managed to jam the plug into the outlet and moved the switch from "off" to "on," the mike wouldn't work. These things never worked for me. Sure enough. After a lengthy wrestling match with plug, outlet, and mike, I dared to try it out: "Hello … testing … hello …." Did my voice echo off the roof and walls of the empty room? No, it did not.

"I knew it!" I exclaimed with something akin to triumph, feeling both angry and frustrated, yet strangely gratified that my prophesy had been fulfilled. Electronic equipment never functions for me; therefore, the mike hadn't let me down.

I paced the front of the church, bemoaning my bad luck under my breath, and beginning to feel anxiety over how I would make the service go smoothly without a second microphone. Then I stomped over behind the pulpit, flicked the main power switch, and tested the main mike that I'd use throughout the service.

"Well, at least I have one microphone that works."

Then, as if turning on that main power switch had also activated my brain, it hit me. Could it possibly be . . . ?

I strode purposefully back across the front of the church to the free-standing microphone and again moved the switch to "on." It worked! All it needed was power, of course.

Often we expect things to go wrong — and wish for them to go wrong so we can gain the satisfaction of proving ourselves right. We can apparently even will things to go wrong as long as it means we can take pride in having correctly predicted the outcome — especially if we predict it will be negative. I was aware of feeling smug when, just as I thought, the secondary mike didn't work. Perhaps my prediction gave me the illusion of power in a powerless situation when it came true.

It's clear to me, as I wrap up this article, what I could have done differently in order to avoid panic and frustration, although it would also have deprived me of that sweet self-righteousness. Instead of kneeling in the church sanctuary trying to force things to go my way and expecting they wouldn't, I would've been better off to kneel there that Sunday morning and turn the control over to God.

——

Problems cannot be solved at the same level of awareness that created them.

— Albert Einstein

Planning Myself Out Of A Good Time

Proverbs 16:1

The plans of the mind belong to mortals,
but the answer of the tongue is from the Lord.

---

*I*t was already about 9:00 in the evening by the time we'd found the place. The reason we did find it is because one of my companions, the driver of the vehicle, needed to heed the call of nature at a downtown Edmonton gas station. While in the building, he thought to make an inquiry regarding a good restaurant. He received this answer: "There's a great Italian spot just on the corner there."

So here we were, in a modern decor that boasted mustard-yellow walls, metallic furnishings, dim candle light, and a stone-tiled floor. In one corner a young woman strummed her acoustic guitar while softly singing folksy-sounding songs.

And the food! I have never had such delicious pasta. I ordered the seafood linguini tossed in a garlic, olive oil and white wine sauce. When the waiter returned with my glass of wine and my heaping plate, I was delighted to discover that the mussels and clams scattered on the noodles were still in their shells. I surpassed not only my own expectations but those of my companions and the waiter by eating the whole works — more food than I usually consume in a week!

Now I've something to admit of which I'm not very proud. Truth is, I didn't want to eat downtown during our weekend away. I had no desire to drive around and around, uncertain of our destination and of when, where, or what we would finally eat. No, I wanted to plan it all out and neatly organize a meal in a generic chain restaurant conveniently located near our west-end hotel at a time predetermined by a carefully-made reservation. That's my idea of good time.

Boy, am I glad I didn't get my way and that my predictably boring, stale evening was thwarted by my stubborn friends' sense of adventure and their refusal to be restricted by a reservation. Sigh. Another lesson learned at a small expense to my pride. It's true. I am proud of my ability to organize and control time, to drain the excitement and spontaneity out of any situation. It comforts me to believe that I usually know what's going to happen next because I've set it up that way. Perhaps this tendency not, only comes from my personality but also from a school teacher. My entire life has evolved to resemble long-range plans.

Perhaps I waste much time attempting to drive my life in what I believe to be the appropriate direction when, apparently, life often turns out okay whether my controlling hands are on the reins or not. And as in the case of our weekend in Edmonton it sometimes turns out better when I drop those reins and hand them over to a little adventure.

Who knows? There may be other gifts of God placed intentionally for my enjoyment that I neglect as a result of my need to control. Also, there may be important tasks set in my path that I carelessly step over without even seeing because I am so wrapped up in controlling what I'll eat, what I'll wear, how others will perceive me. What a waste of energy!

Experiences like discovering that incredible restaurant in a place I didn't initially want to go cause me to consider what we unwittingly deprive ourselves of when we seek to control, organize, and drive ourselves into worry. I realize (and I've mentioned this many times before) that I not only deprive myself of some of life's sweetest pleasures through the art of worry, but also I harm myself with toils and struggles that unnecessarily tire both mind and body. And today, with the taste of pasta and red wine still lingering on memory's tongue, I'm seriously planning a change.

Life is what happens when you are making other plans.

— John Lennon

Cookies Don't Lie

Psalm 90:12

So teach us to count our days
that we may gain a wise heart.

The other day, I ordered some take-out Chinese food. You know, not real Chinese food but Western-style Chinese food. Everything fried and battered. I call it "deep-fried fat," and sometimes I just really enjoy it.

So I got the Chinese food home, made myself comfortable in front of the television and dug in, savouring every greasy bite. Stuffed, I finally slumped back deep into the couch with a satisfied sigh. It was then I noticed the fortune cookie sitting on the coffee table alone and doing a poor job of hiding in its clear cellophane wrapper. It might have done a better job had it known that its fate was to be the same as the egg rolls' and chicken balls' that came before. That fortune cookie sure didn't possess a lot of foresight.

Uncomfortably, I made the long stretch to reach the fortune cookie and resumed my relaxed position as soon as it was in my grip. I peeled away the plastic and bit the cookie in two.

"But wait!" I thought as I chewed. "Something's missing." There was no slim paper fortune sticking out from the remaining half of the cookie. Having not yet swallowed, I searched my mouth frantically with my tongue beginning to fear the worst: my stomach lining would be the one to read my fortune. Search as they may, the taste bud posse did not locate any paper pulp in the sugar and flour there in my mouth, so with one mighty gulp I sent the mixture on the rest of its journey with confidence.

Still, I was left without a fortune. A little disappointed, I munched the second half of the cookie pondering what it meant not to have a fortune. I mean, I've gotten two or even three in one cookie before, but never have I gotten none!

"If you don't have a fortune," I wondered despondently, "do you even have a future? What dark news has this cookie brought?"

Then, as my mood gradually lightened, I began to see that the lack of a fortune is not an evil omen but a sign of freedom. It's like God and the cosmos saying, "This thing called life is yours to design and do with as you will. No slip of paper in a cookie purchased at a Chinese food restaurant will determine your destiny. You write your own fortune."

Instead of searching for wisdom in a crunchy shell, I was given the freedom to look inside myself for it, to determine my fortune and my future. I can steer myself toward "success in my business dealings" and "time invested in friendships." It's up to me to decide whether I "spend more time with my family" or "excel in the workplace." The decision is mine to "pray every day" or "go on a spending spree while funds available." That's what the cookie told me by telling me nothing — and cookies don't lie.

———

I couldn't wait for success ... so I went ahead without it.

— Jonathon Winters

To Trust A Snorkeler

John 21:4–8

Just after daybreak, Jesus stood on the beach; but the disciples did not know that it was Jesus. Jesus said to them, "Children, you have no fish, have you?" They answered him, "No." He said to them, "Cast the net to the right side of the boat, and you will find some." So they cast it, and now they were not able to haul it in because there were so many fish. That disciple whom Jesus loved said to Peter, "It is the Lord!" When Simon Peter heard that it was the Lord, he put on some clothes, for he was naked, and jumped into the sea. But the other disciples came in the boat, dragging the net full of fish, for they were not far from the land, only about a hundred yards off.

---

*I*t was a pretty average morning of fishing. Two or three other boats dotted the little lake and, although it was light out, the sun had not yet shown herself above the tree line. Water bugs of various sizes and shapes flitted over the water's still surface. It was these we followed, hoping that where there are bugs, there must be hungry fish. And so quietly we moved along, one paddling, one trolling, no one speaking.

It went on like this for a peaceful hour or so. From the canoe I stared deep into the lake, trying to spot fish as they swam through the less-than-clear, greenish water. I suspect it was because I was focusing so hard on trout-spotting that I nearly jumped out of my skin when a creature in a wet-suit and snorkel mask suddenly emerged, proclaiming, "There's lots of fish over there!" It pointed enthusiastically to the shoreline as my heart threatened to beat out of my chest.

Nobody snorkels in a tiny man-made lake! The snorkeler was so out of place that at first my companion and I could not register what had appeared after soundlessly swimming alongside our boat.

It reminded me of the morning Jesus appeared to his disciples on the beach at the Sea of Tiberias. Of course, Jesus' appearance was unexpected as he had been crucified and buried. The disciples didn't recognize their master because he was so out of place. He asked them if they had caught any fish and when they answered No he instructed them, "Cast the net to the right side of the boat, and you will find some."

We finally recognized the snorkeler for who he was because of his knowledge of what we could not see. In the same way the disciples recognized Jesus because of his knowledge of what they could not see.

It's about trust, I think. The disciples trusted Jesus *before* they recognized him. They trusted the man they thought was a stranger and he led them to find the fish they needed to survive. By his knowledge they knew him — but they had to trust him first.

Neither friends nor family nor Jesus can lead us to salvation until we are willing to trust. Upon building that trust, we will then be able to recognize who can save us and will.

Trust everybody, but cut the cards.

— Finley Peter Dunne

Dental Meltdown

Mark 15:33–36

When it was noon, darkness came over the whole land until three in the afternoon. At three o'clock Jesus cried out with a loud voice, "Eloi, Eloi, lema sabachthani?" which means, "My God, my God, why have you forsaken me?" When some of the bystanders heard it, they said, "Listen, he is calling for Elijah." And someone ran, filled a sponge with sour wine, put it on a stick, and gave it to him to drink, saying, "Wait, let us see whether Elijah will come to take him down."

———

I clung to the chair as if it were seat 4A of a crashing plane. My hands gripped the armrests so hard that my fingerprints are still visible in the padded vinyl, and I sat so rigidly that I think a disc or two of my spinal column may have been crushed. Sweat beaded on my skin and was absorbed by my suddenly sticky clothing. The only comfort came in the form of the words spoken just prior to my trial: this should only take about twenty minutes.

Only. Twenty minutes tap dancing on burning coals, twenty minutes warding off a lion attack, twenty minutes in a crashing plane. Little comfort — but some. This wouldn't last forever. So with my frozen face feeling like an over-inflated beach ball and my mouth pried open, I was confronting my worst fear: the dentist's chair.

The unnerving, high-pitched whir of God-knows-what made my heart quadruple its beats per minute. Above me, beyond the white light's glare, the dentist and assistant discussed office stuff and my mouth alternately. It was all pretty much an auditory blur until I heard some words that stood out like an electric guitar in a chamber music performance.

"Do you smell that?"

"What?"

"That. It's not burning, is it?"

"Oh my." Alarmed. "It could be.... I hope not."

"What's burning?!" my mind screamed in terror as my imagination pictured orange flames leaping from my mouth in a sort of dental meltdown. Every muscle in my body tensed to the point of nearly snapping like carelessly tightened guitar strings.

"I'll go check on it."

Confusion followed by some relief. If she had to leave the room to see what was burning, chances increased that it wasn't anything in my mouth. My muscles relaxed slightly.

The assistant strode back in.

"How is it?"

"The chicken's fine. Just really hot, that's all."

Chicken! They were cooking up a batch of chicken in the back for the office staff to enjoy together. Nothing was on fire in my mouth. Shortly after this realization, my dental appointment was over and I was on my way, numb and shaky but with teeth neatly filled.

Misunderstandings in stressful situations are common and cause a wide range of emotion. In my case, misunderstanding caused gut-wrenching, weak-in-the-knees trepidation followed by relief. The onlookers at the base of Jesus' cross felt smug satisfaction in their misinterpretation of his words and the need to dare him to hope — and this in a situation where hope was nowhere to be found.

Our misunderstandings don't, thank goodness, affect an event's outcome. They merely have an impact on our reaction to it. I was scared because I thought somehow something in my mouth was burning and some of the people present at Jesus' death felt smug at his helplessness. But nothing was on fire (not even lunch) and, in the end, Jesus conquered death. Our misconceptions don't alter reality — only our perception of it. Good thing, too, because dentistry should never, no matter how illogically terrified we are, involve fire.

We see things not as they are, but as we are.

— H. M. Tomlinson

Mistaken Identity

1 Samuel 25:25

My lord, do not take seriously this ill-natured fellow, Nabal;
for as his name is, so is he; Nabal is his name, and folly is
with him.

———

*T*he other day a couple of my friends and I were in a restaurant on Edmonton's south side having some lunch and a good visit. Everything was progressing as it should in an eating establishment at noon. The place was nearly full, and serving staff decked out in uniforms bustled pleasantly between tables full of patrons. Platters of amazing-smelling food were carried by and our order was taken amidst the dull noise of the busy place.

It was my friend who spotted and pointed out to me the most interesting one of all. He nodded toward a big, bald, burly waiter, carrying a tray and sporting a flowery Hawaiian shirt like his co-workers. So far nothing out of the ordinary until ….

"Hey, what does that guy's nametag say?"

I squinted in the man's direction trying to pick out the white tag in the colourful garden which was his shirt.

"Sarah."

Yup. Sarah. Now that is an interesting detail! We sat for a little while pondering why this young, strong man would be christened Sarah. Was it something like the story Johnny Cash tells regarding a certain boy named Sue? Perhaps he was given the name to toughen him up in a world that would surely treat him rough.

The mystery was solved for me when a waitress passed the man apparently named Sarah and said, "Hey, Scott!"

Oh! So Scott was like the rest of us sometimes are. I can't say for sure that this is how it went, but I wouldn't be surprised if I'm right: Scott's alarm went off on time but he had stayed up far too late again and so by the time he dragged himself out of bed, rapidly shaved, dawned his summery shirt and brushed the fuzz from his teeth, he was pretty much late for work already. And as is usually the case when we're late, his windshield still bore a thick layer of early-morning frost that needed to be scraped, and the traffic was just a bit heavier than usual.

He ran into work from the far end of the parking lot — the only place he'd been able to find a spot — and grabbed the first name tag he saw bearing his initial "S." Hence, a frazzled Scott became an efficient waitress called Sarah.

Scott and his mismatched nametag made me think of how the way we perceive ourselves can differ so much from the way others see us. To Scott, he's just Scott and, as far as he knows, the thick white strip of plastic pinned to his shirt confirms this. But to my friends and me, Scott is a man named Sarah.

I wonder how often what I'm showing the world matches the real me, the soul that resides under the clothes I choose to wear and the make-up and skin. It depends. Sometimes I'm convinced the essential me shines through and no one could possibly miss it. Other times, I wrap my soul in a thick cloak of fear and insecurity to protect me when I'm feeling vulnerable or mistrusting. Then not even my closest friends can recognize who I may really be.

But God always knows. That's why it's important to keep that connection. If we fail to recognize ourselves, we can turn to God wherein the real self lies. The clothes may be a uniform and the nametag may be inaccurate, but through our relationship with the Creator, our true selves are revealed.

God will become visible as God's image is reborn in you.

— St. Bernard of Clairveux

Your Spiritual Key Ring

Ezekiel 38:7

Be ready and keep ready, you and all the companies that are
assembled around you, and hold yourselves in reserve for
them.

———

*O*nce again I entered the secretary's office in the morning after
having walked the length of the hall to find my door locked.

"Morning. Can I borrow your keys again? Door's locked."

"Don't you have keys?"

"Nope."

"I thought I gave some to you at the beginning of the year. Are
you sure?"

"Yep."

"Hmm. Portable three, right?"

"Yep."

"Do you have your school keys with you? Let's go up to your
room and figure this out."

"Okay."

So we made our way through the hallway back up to my classroom.

"You try your keys first — just to see if you've got the right one
there."

I pulled my jumble of keys from a pocket in the side of my briefcase, selected the most promising-looking one, slid it into the keyhole
and watched as the knob turned with embarrassing ease.

"Oh," I said, because what else do you say when something like
this happens?

The thing is, I had been depending upon the office keys to gain
access to my classroom when, right there and all along, I had the
means to unlock the door. There had been books I could've picked
up in the evening and brought home, bits of marking and organizing
that could've potentially gotten done, but I believed I couldn't get

into the room, so these little tasks never got completed. How convenient for me.

The discovery of the key that worked now confronted me with that most dreaded of burdens: responsibility.

You see, before the discovery, I was able to blame my inaction on external factors. But having control means having responsibility, and having responsibility allows freedom. Suddenly I had the freedom to move in and out of my classroom when I wanted to. Hmm.

How often we depend upon others to provide us with the resources we don't believe we have. We get our spouse to highway drive or cook because we're sure we can't. We hire an interior decorator or landscape designer because we lack confidence in our own sense of what looks good. We balk at travelling or shopping or going skating alone because we feel we need companionship to engage in these activities.

And sometimes, we wait for someone to bring God's word or God's will to us. Is it possible that we have the resources right there in our hearts to reach God ourselves through prayer and meditation? Could it be that deep within our souls lies the potential to commune with God and that all we need to do is admit that we were given the key a while ago? If the answer is Yes, we can enjoy the freedom of finding God for ourselves.

It's so easy to assume that we can't unlock the door that stands between us and a relationship with the Creator. Suddenly realizing that we can is a little scary but also pretty exciting. If you're wanting to gain some freedom and take on some responsibility for knowing God, check your spiritual key ring and find out if you already carrying around the equipment to do so.

Destiny is as destiny does. If you believe you have no control, then you have no control.

— Wess Roberts

Going
Deep

Catch Me If You Can

I fled Him, down the nights and down the days;
I fled Him, down the arches of the years;
I fled Him, down the labyrinthine ways
Of my own mind; and in the midst of tears
I hid from Him, and under running laughter.
Up vistaed hopes I sped;
And shot, precipitated,
Adown Titanic glooms of chasmed fears,
From those strong feet that followed, followed after.
But with unhurrying chase,
And unperturbed pace,
Deliberate speed, majestic instancy,
They beat — and a Voice beat
More instant than the Feet —
"All things betray thee, who betrayest Me."

— from "The Hound of Heaven" by Francis Thompson

---

*R*ecently I sat alone in the dark and called upon God, and as I did, a wave of guilt washed over me leaving me feeling soaked with hypocrisy. It wasn't with the intention of praising God for all the good things I've got that I prayed. Nor was it a prayer of mercy and compassion for those who are suffering under the weight of poverty, despair, disease, or starvation. I didn't pray for justice nor did I pray for the comfort of those serving prison time for voicing their political views or for writing books.

My prayer was for me: "God, help me." Even as I uttered my desperate prayer I thought about the self-serving motivation and was right there and then inclined to cease praying.

Instead, I continued to beg for solace but finished up with a little praise for what I recognized as my many blessings.

We're human and I suppose that's why this happens. When life is going smoothly and events feel mostly under our control and reasonably predictable, we don't feel the need for God in quite the same way as we do when faced with an x-ray we don't completely understand accompanied by a doctor's grim countenance, which explains the picture better than the picture itself, or when the police call at three in the morning, or when a commercial airplane crashes into the side of a building in New York City.

It's then we cry out. And often, I think, we feel guilty for seeming to approach God only when we need something that this world can't supply us with. We come seeking comfort, a reason, a miracle.

My point is that it's better to approach God with our own needs than to not show up at all. It is possible that we are welcomed by the Creator under any circumstance as loving parents would welcome home children hard hit by unemployment, or financially stable kids bringing home that first grandchild. They're just happy to see them on the doorstep, safe at home at last.

Sometimes our need stemming from pain merely opens the door to a relationship with God. Like any relationship, if it is healthy it will grow beyond that initial self-serving need into something more balanced, something extending beyond self.

You may arrive on an elderly neighbour's doorstep one spring day to borrow half a cup of sugar and end up staying for tea and cookies. And then, as spring opens up into summer you may find yourself on her patio a couple of times a week enjoying sunshine and iced tea, a relationship having sprung from the need of half a cup of sugar.

If the British poet Francis Thompson was right, God pursues us, and in finally coming to God, we end up where we've belonged since our births. That makes me feel somewhat less guilty regarding my motives for coming to God in prayer. Perhaps the reason isn't as important as the action.

Begin somewhere.
You cannot build a reputation on what you *intend* to do.

— Liz Smith

Enjoy the Journey

Deuteronomy 34:4–5

The Lord said to him, "This is the land of which I swore
to Abraham, to Isaac, and to Jacob, saying, 'I will give it
to your descendants'; I have let you see it with your eyes,
but you shall not cross over there." Then Moses, the
servant of the Lord, died there in the land of Moab, at
the Lord's command.

———

*Y*ou know what response drives me crazy when I ask someone to
go for a walk? "Where are we walking to?"

It drives me crazy because a walk isn't about where we're walking
to — it's all about enjoying the weather, the exercise, one another's
company. Who cares where we end up as long as it's eventually back
home? What happens in between is the joy of the journey.

"Just enjoy the journey!" is my wise counsel to a walking partner
who needs to be going somewhere. If that doesn't work, I promise a
destination of interest, such as an ice cream stand or music store.
Then we're on our way.

Having made this complaint, I have to admit that, although I'm
very good at enjoying a walking adventure, I'm no good at savouring
the scenery in walks of life! In too many ways I am a severely goal-
oriented person.

Talk about paying lip-service! I dash about from one task to another, completing chores like knocking over bowling pins, but I never
pause to rejoice in the score. Instead, I reset the pins and challenge
myself anew, trying to see how many pins I can knock over in a single
day. Is anyone else on my team? Who cares! I'm not here to make
friends, drink beer, and eat salty pretzels. And I wish they'd turn that
music down. It's distracting me from my goal. (Yikes! Where'd the
bowling analogy come from? I don't bowl. I don't even want to bowl.)

Constantly struggling to reach that elusive place where I'll finally be satisfied with work, looks, and social life is tiring me out. I've only myself to blame — I acknowledge that. But how do I change from being a destination person into a woman who appreciates the travelling? I would like to be someone who watches out the window for deer in the hayfields the way I did as a journey-enjoying kid. There's hope there: striving to fulfill stiff self-expectations may be a learned behaviour. Well, folks, it's time to do a little unlearning.

In pondering this, I thought that it might help to look at people I love and admire for being who they are, even though they haven't attained fame or a modelling contract. I also turned to the Bible for examples of heroes such as Moses, who spent his life leading God's chosen people to the Promised Land. If he had been a guy concerned too heavily with destination, he would have thought his life pointless at the very end when God says, "Thanks for your work, but you won't set foot in this land you've walked toward for all your life." Somehow, I think he was a journey type of guy who, at one hundred and twenty years old, was probably grateful beyond words just to lie down without having to worry about getting up again.

It's possible that the joy of the journey, not achieving the goals we set for ourselves, is God's intended gift to us. Maybe we're good enough for the Creator if we choose to read in a backyard lawn chair or to take four more courses toward our Master's degree — as long as, in doing either, we thank God for the time we're given and taste the sweetness in each moment.

The aim of life is to live, and to live means to be aware, joyously, serenely, divinely aware.

— Henry Miller

Praying Around the Bush

Jeremiah 33:3

Call to me and I will answer you, and will tell you great and
hidden things that you have not known.

———

*M*y aunt and I shared a pleasant telephone conversation the other
day, during part of which we discussed the nature of prayer. I
was in the midst of making a difficult decision and feeling unsure
about what outcome would best serve.God.

My aunt: Well, I'll pray for you.

Me: Thanks, but please don't pray for anything too specific because I can't tell what God wants me to do.

My aunt: Okay then. I'll pray around the bush.

I laughed. Pray around the bush! That's funny — and a great
description of prayer offered for a non-specific outcome. So often,
we are tempted to inform the Creator exactly what it is that we need
to make us happy, to make us rich, to make us loved.

"All right, God, just do this little thing for me and it'll be wonderful. I know exactly what I need. Trust me."

Trouble with this kind of plea is that the supplicant is not taking
into consideration the will of God. Someone might pray, for example, for a job in a corner office when the real meaning to their thus-far
hollow existence lies in teaching school in Africa. Another may be
down on his knees in the cathedral begging for acceptance into law
school when what's important to God is that he plays his guitar in
the subway station. A woman kneels on the kitchen floor and, closing her swelling and bruising eyes, praying that her marriage may be
restored to a place of safety. God sighs sadly because the woman must
leave the marriage in order to find the gentle man who waits for her
outside the confines of that abusive relationship.

Of course, we're always going to pray without knowledge of God's
will. Given the narrow scope of our humanness, it's all we can do.

The key is to continue our prayers but also to increase our awareness of what we can't know, to understand that we are unable to see around the corners of time. It may be advisable to end off with "your will be done."

It felt safe to have my aunt "pray around the bush" for me. The thing is, our view of the Big Picture is so limited that we can't possibly know what's best for us in the short run, and we certainly can't know the will of God. The best we can do under most circumstances is to pray around the bush.

Go ahead and ask for those outcomes that you truly desire. It can't hurt as long as we remember within our prayers to take into account God's will. Then, no matter what happens, we'll have the assurance of helping to bring to realization God's kingdom on earth.

—

I beg you to have patience with everything unresolved in your heart
and try to love the questions themselves as if they were locked rooms
or books written in a very foreign language.
Don't search for the answers, which could not be given you now,
because you would not be able to live them.
And the point is, to live everything.
Live the questions now.
Perhaps then, someday far in the future, you will gradually, without ever noticing it, live your way into the answer.

— Rainer Maria Rilke

This Little Light Of Mine

Luke 1:76–79

And you, child, will be called the prophet of the Most High;
for you will go before the Lord to prepare his ways, to give
knowledge of salvation to his people by the forgiveness of
their sins. By the tender mercy of our God, the dawn on
high will break upon us, to give light to those who sit in
darkness and in the shadow of death, to guide our feet
into the way of peace.

———

*J*ust the other day I lit a couple of candles around the house to
help ward off the newly-extending darkness of winter. For the
first hour or so they burned brightly, casting rings of light and catching tall, shivering shadows in their glow. Then, suddenly and without warning, the light dimmed so drastically that the shadows deepened, almost blending in with the surrounding darkness, and ceased to move at all.

I thought to myself, "Self, what's going on with these candles? They're brand-new! Surely they shouldn't be so dim so soon."

I walked over to one candle. There, in a deep pool of red, rose-reminiscent wax, barely burned a tiny blue flame looking as if it would surely drown if the puddle rose any more. I poured the excess wax from the candleholder and immediately the flame leaped up high. Now the shadows danced to life and the whole room seemed to light up.

The resurrected candle flame reminded me of the human soul and how it tends to wane, leap to life, then burn low again. And as with the candle's wax, it's the soul "build-up" that surrounds and then nearly drowns us, causing our light to flicker low.

Let me explain. I can picture our souls as the vessels for all our hopes and dreams, fears and dreads. All our thoughts, emotions, and memories accumulate within us and then, occasionally, it all becomes too much. The level rises, threatening to smother the light emitted by our souls. It is then that we need to pour ourselves out to God in prayer, to rid ourselves of all the stuff we gather through daily living and through our thoughts and actions. Without this outlet, there is a possibility that our light could flicker out.

Then when we are poured out, our light shines brighter than ever, reaching into the most remote corners and revealing those things perhaps not noticed before. When we neglect to pour out our souls and allow that flame to rejuvenate, God's light is less able to shine through us and our souls are less able to do the job they were created to do: illuminate God's will and presence.

We need to maintain our souls through prayer and meditation if we are to serve God and God's world to our fullest potential. Like those candles that can burn beautifully if looked after, so can our souls if we take the time to make sure that nothing is causing our flame to burn low.

We are all meant to shine as children do.
We are born to manifest the glory of God that is within us.
It is not just in some of us; it is in everyone.
And as we let our light shine, we unconsciously give other people permission to do the same.
As we are liberated from our own fear, our presence automatically releases others.

— Marianne Williamson from
A Return To Love

Sometimes Faith Is Not Accepting the Reason

Ecclesiastes 8:10–13

Then I saw the wicked buried; they used to go in and out of the holy place, and were praised in the city where they had done such things. This also is vanity. Because sentence against an evil deed is not executed speedily, the human heart is fully set to do evil. Though sinners do evil a hundred times and prolong their lives, yet I know that it will be well with those who fear God, because they stand in fear before him, but it will not be well for the wicked, neither will they prolong their days like a shadow, because they do not stand in fear before God.

---

*W*e were sitting around one of those early summer evenings, the conversation and camaraderie flowing as freely as the wine, when talk veered in the direction of the meaning of life and got stuck in that ditch for a while. My friends summed up human existence this way: "Everything happens for a reason."

"I'm not sure," I responded tentatively. Eyes grew wide and I felt the need to explain myself. "I can't imagine that Ethiopian babies dying of dehydration at six months old is part of God's master plan."

Does this seem like a faithless statement? It was necessary to explain my position to my friends and now I'll do so the best I can without the added eloquence supplied by wine to explain it to you — explain how it argues in favour of faith.

Sometimes events take place that are spiritually shattering. I don't believe that the woman whose husband is tortured to death, and whose body she watches being doused in gasoline and set afire, is ever able to console her devastated spirit with, "Everything happens for a reason." Oh, she knows it's true. The reason is political injustice and the denial of human rights in her country. That's why her young, strong husband, who joined in the fight for freedom from oppression, met with a horrifying death. Everything happens for a reason indeed.

Is she faithless because she cannot see how this fits into the Creator's plan? I think that if she could understand this as God's will, she would be inclined to hate the master of the plan. But she's not faithless. Instead of shrinking into despair and burning with hatred, she will give reason to her husband's death through her own life by how she chooses to act thereafter.

And so, risking her own life, she takes in political dissidents and hides them for nights at a time, feeding them warm food and encouraging words to give them the strength that seems impossible to maintain in the face of such odds. She teaches her children that the system ruling over them is wrong, and she teaches them how to survive in that system so that one day they may change it and live to see those changes.

Giving meaning to catastrophic events is how we promote faith in action. The young wife could accept no God-given reason for her husband's violent death, but because she lived her faith afterwards, his death was not in vain. When we can admit that we don't know why things happen, that some things are meaningless and that evil clearly exists, faith isn't absent. That's when it becomes crucial.

Giving meaning to happenings is in itself an act of faith. Conversely, I believe that accepting injustice and violence because "everything happens for a reason" breeds inaction and is dangerous faithlessness.

We could know all possible knowledge, and all of theology and all the things about God, but we would not be able to light a fire in the hearts of the people. We could just be uttering words, not living those words. That is why it is necessary for us that our words be the fruit of our life, the fruit of our prayers.

— Mother Teresa

Painful Gain

Mark 4:1–2

Then Jesus was led up by the Spirit into the wilderness
to be tempted by the devil. He fasted forty days and forty
nights, and afterwards he was famished.

---

*N*o pain, no gain? Not always. But sometimes the pain is definitely unavoidable. Rats. I wish it weren't true.

Many times in the course of our lives we are faced with the choice of giving up something that we are enjoying for a short time, yet knowing that in the long run, it's hurting us. You know the stuff I mean. Doctors continually warn us about the fat that will inevitably narrow and clog our arteries, and yet we continue to scarf down potato chips and fried chicken as if there were no tomorrow. We realize that our frenzied consumption of pure unadulterated fat will probably cause that final tomorrow to arrive a little earlier. Still it's so hard to let those deliciously crunchy snack foods go, even knowing that following the initial pain of separation, we'd be better off without them.

The benefits of exercise to our bodies and minds is no mystery. We are fully aware that walking or swimming or going to the gym is far better for us than either being sucked into the couch's force field or working ourselves into a trembling exhaustion that leaves us sleepless with worry over what didn't get accomplished. A bit of physical activity goes a long way to improve the quality of everyday life and to maybe even lengthen that life a little. Yet we are less inclined to take it up as part of our routines than we are to take home more paper work or spend more time on the couch.

Most of us have been in relationships that we know are harmful. Although we cling to them because of the comfort and familiarity they provide, we feel that they're eating away at us from the inside, one tiny painful piece at a time. It's then we need to decide if it's necessary to break ties or if we can afford to keep on sacrificing some of who we are.

Good changes that bring long-term benefits are often painful. (This is a bit of a turn-around, I know, as I'm usually preaching living in the moment; but please bear with me — it ends up there.) But not taking the plunge into temporary discomfort could place us on the path toward permanent danger to our physical or psychological health or to our spirits.

I doubt that Jesus was greatly looking forward to entering the desert following his baptism when he had received confirmation as God's son along with a blessing. Now that was a comfortable place, but the Son of God wasn't permitted to stay there for long. God needed him to go to a place of painful growth so that he could move forward into his ministry with the strength and self-knowledge to live each moment of each day as God would have him. (See. I told you it'd come back to living in the moment. It has to, because that's when everything happens.)

So if something's giving you a short-term reward but keeping you from long-term success or fulfillment, take a closer look at it and see if you can survive extricating yourself from it. No, it's not easy, but perhaps the most painful changes are the ones most worthwhile.

You must do the thing you think you cannot do.

— Eleanor Roosevelt

Stuck In the Wilderness

Mark 1:12–14

And the Spirit immediately drove him out into the
wilderness. He was in the wilderness forty days, tempted
by Satan; and he was with the wild beasts; and the
angels waited on him.

I am in a strange yet familiar place right now. We've all been there.
I'm stuck in the wilderness.

A short while ago, I was really busy with work, with my studies,
a wedding to attend in B.C., a meeting in Edmonton, and a little
volunteer work to top it off. Put simply, May was hectic! All through
that crazy month I never took a second to glance ahead from where I
was at the time. If I had taken a moment to turn the calendar page to
June, I would've seen that everything filling my world was going to
come to a sudden, simultaneous end — just like that! And that I
would be left teetering on the dangerous edge of not knowing what
to do with my time or mind.

Unlike my consciousness, my body must've seen the end coming. It was obviously exhausted from my busy stint, and as soon as I
finished up my final commitment, it told me so in the form of a sore
throat, pounding headache, and runny nose. It was in this state that
I entered the long stretch of doing nothingness accompanied by a
Kleenex box, glasses of orange juice and cups of herbal tea, and a
novel I'd been wanting to read for a long time. When I wasn't sleep-
ing, I was either reading or just thinking — definitely moving at a
much different speed at the end of May than at the start.

As a product of our adrenaline-rushed society, I feel predictably
guilty in my immobile state and often on the verge of panic, wondering if I will ever re-enter life. Of course I will, but when we're lost in
the wilderness, life's paths become elusive and we begin to question
whether we have the faith, the strength, or the skills to find our way out.

Perhaps that's why we need our time alone in the wilderness, confronted by our doubts and questions. It can serve as our turn-around time. It is time alone: there's no one else in my life currently experiencing the exact same wilderness that I am. They may be dealing with a similar doubt, a similar fear, or a guilt like mine, but there's no one trapped in the same place I am. My wilderness is my own.

I think that Jesus needed to enter the wilderness before he could go out into the world and do what he was born to do. The time he spent in the wilderness served as his turn-around time. We don't know for sure what Jesus did as an adult prior to his active ministry. Some scholars speculate that he probably worked in the same line of work as his father. It's possible that, like many of us, he was pretty comfortable working every day to make a living. Yet something compelled him to take on the responsibility of changing the world.

Notice: like most of us, Jesus didn't decide on his own to wander out into the wilderness in order to choose life's course. "The Spirit drove him out...." This phrase and the use of the word "drove" convinces me that Jesus was fairly content with his life's work before he began his ministry and, if not completely content, at least a bit reluctant to make a huge change and to take on a huge task.

That's most likely the reason the majority of us find ourselves it the wilderness. It's time to change, and often we're not ready to do so. Didn't we just get used to life's steady rhythm, it's predictable pace? Why can't that hidden potential deep within just stay hidden? Why, all of a sudden, does it so desperately need our attention?

Beats me. All I know is I'm back in this place for the time being and, if I want out any time soon, I'd better keep my eyes focused on the future and my heart focused on my soul. Then, with luck or destiny on my side, God's will will become clear and point the way out of the desert.

———

Wisdom is knowing what path to take next ...
integrity is taking it.

— Robyn Elprehzleinn

A Whole Lotta Winter

Proverbs 20:27

The human spirit is the lamp of
the Lord,
searching every inmost part.

When it came to writing this January piece for my newspaper
column, I sure wasn't inspired. With Christmas and New Year's
past, taking with them their inflated stories and leaving my imagination feeling empty and flat, I didn't know what to write about. The
January blues — not much ahead but a whole lotta winter.

But life needs to continue. It would be great if we could simply
call in to work and say, "Sorry, I won't be in today. I'm just not feeling all that inspired." But that's not the way it goes.

Last Monday, following a glorious holiday of feasting and study-
ing, I was faced with the inevitable return to work. This is always
tough even if you've got a great job (as I do) and really enjoy your
work. As that final weekend of vacation dissolved into the first week
of work, the inspiration to go back refreshed and renewed just didn't
happen. Somehow I thought it would begin like a gentle snowfall on
Sunday afternoon and by Monday morning, I'd be wrapped in a shining white blanket of energy and enthusiasm. Yeah, right.

By Sunday afternoon I was getting pretty desperate for some inspiration and since waiting for it to fall from the sky hadn't panned
out, I decided to try another tactic: I would attempt to search for it
myself. I relentlessly mined brain and heart, chipping here and there
at the solid walls around my imagination, but the yellow circle of
light cast by the lamp on my helmet picked out only stale ideas,
dreary outlooks, and a few rocky outcroppings of doubts. I was about
to give up when, way over there in the deepest darkest recess, hud-
dled and forgotten in a corner, I spied a little inspiration.

It wasn't a big inspiration, but it was far more than I'd expected to find on my own, and it was all I needed. Carefully I brought it out of the dark, and in the light above ground it quickly grew.

It told me to focus on what I loved most about my job and advised that I do a couple of things on Monday that would most involve those aspects. It was that easy! So by Sunday night I had discovered and raised that little inspiration placed there by God as a treasure for me to find if only I was willing to look for it.

This encounter with inspiration made me see it a little differently. Perhaps inspiration isn't something that always appears magically (though it's undeniably sweet when it does) but more a matter of give and take. The ability to experience inspiration is a gift given to us at birth, and uncountable opportunities to taste it are presented throughout our lifetimes.

But when we are not presented with external inspiration, maybe God expects us to work at finding it internally. Maybe God enjoys seeing us act resourcefully and creatively. I imagine the scenario to be somewhat like parents hiding gifts or planting Easter eggs with the hope that their children will take joy in the discovery as well as in the gift itself.

I'm not saying it's going to be easy as the deepest part of winter falls upon us to find the inspiration that lies within, but even knowing that it's there is a comforting thought. So hold on tight, folks. Winter's here to stay, but I'm convinced we have in ourselves that tiny spark of inspiration to light our way if only we bring it out of the dark.

Those who enter the gates of heaven are not beings who
have no passions
or who have curbed the passions, but those who have
cultivated an understanding of them.

— William Blake

Time: A Non-renewable Resource

Job 8:9

Our days upon earth are a shadow.

After years of teaching school, my father finally retired in June. His colleagues, sad to see him go, bid him a fond farewell with a party and a watch. The school district, pleased with his years of service, put on a dinner in honour of him and the other retirees and presented him with a clock. When we were discussing these gifts, Dad joked, "Do they think I'm not already very aware of the passing of time? 'Here — have some time pieces so you can keep closer track of the hours slipping away.'"

Upon retiring and completing what he views as his life's work, he has not quite decided how to fill the hours and days left to him, but he hopes the answer will come soon.

On the other hand, I have a friend who can't keep track of the passing of time even though his life depends on it. To him time is a magically elastic thing to be overstuffed and stretched, and he is often surprised to find that it has its bounds. For example, he will be planning to start a project and when I point out that it's already 10:00 in the evening, he seems hurt, betrayed by time, disappointed that he can't cram one last thing into the day.

According to the number of watches he owns, this guy should be right on top of time. Watches in various states of repair lie about his place of residence, some waiting for a new battery, some ticking away in want of a functional strap, some beeping every hour perhaps in hopes of being discovered and appreciated. Yet even the watch on his wrist receives very little attention.

Then there's me. I budget time as carefully as I would a canteen of water in the desert. I achieve goals and accomplish a lot in a day, but on the downside, I'm often so worried about wasting time that I completely forget to relax and have fun.

So what is the secret to approaching the passing of time? Do we watch it pass by and wonder where it's going? Do we forget it's there except when its constraints frustrate us? Or do we keep it under a microscope, measured, counted, and never out of our sight? No matter our approach it's crucial to appreciate time, to understand that it is a non-renewable resource.

Time is like politics or religion: everyone chooses the angle that suits them best. But unlike politics or religion, time is ultimately in control: it decides the length of one's life. We can measure time, save time, and waste time, but we cannot escape its movement

In a world where we have learned to control so much of our environment, time remains as untouchable and mysterious as God. We build clocks to hold time and churches to hold God, yet both remain unseen and uncontainable. In a sense, they hold us. We belong in and to the time we are given. Outside of our given time, we were and will be nothing to this earth.

We regard God in as many different ways as we do the passing of time. Some watch God's movement in and over the world, while others sometimes lose track of God completely and then are occasionally surprised when evidence of God reappears. Still others spend so much time and energy focused on matters of heaven that they miss out on the pleasures offered on earth.

The passing of time can serve to remind us of the mysterious, uncontrollable nature of God. We can ponder the existence of God, we can speculate on the mind and will of God, we can contemplate the possibility of eternity and build tall steeples to reach heaven, but we will never contain or fully understand God. Time reminds us that, while we control many things, the One who gave us life and composes our lives remains blessedly beyond our control.

—

What, then, is time? I know well enough what it is, provided that nobody asks me, but if I am asked what it is and try to explain, I am baffled.

— St. Augustine

Making Room For Miracles

Psalm 132:3–5

I will not enter my house or get into my bed;
I will not give sleep to my eyes or slumber to my eyelids,
Until I find a place for the Lord, a dwelling place for the
Mighty One of Jacob.

On a recent trip I had the opportunity to attend a service in a fifteen-pew United Church in Hardisty, Alberta, led by a travelling preacher who, between frequent speaking engagements, provides leadership to smaller congregations who find themselves temporarily without a minister. He is a bold man, unafraid to say out loud the things many of us think. One of these courageous statements sticks out in my mind: Our churches are empty because we don't need God when things are going well.

It made me think. I hear a lot of people say that they don't need to go to church to find God, that God is all around us and not the sole property of churchgoers. I agree. But what do we do to keep us aware that God is all around when we are not engaged in formal, structured worship? I don't know about you, but on some Sunday mornings when I'm not at worship, I am not glorifying in God's presence in me and all about me. Usually I'm catching up on extra jobs from my weekly work that spill into the weekend or doing some mundane task such as vacuuming or doing laundry. Not very holy, eh?

We may be feeling unsuccessful in our search for God in church, but I'm reasonably certain that we're not going to have much more luck looking in the laundry room behind the fabric softener, or in the vacuum cleaner bag, or in the afternoon racket of the shopping mall.

If the Creator did enter into the rush of our lives, would we be quiet and still enough to notice? Or would the divine presence be drowned out by a blaring TV announcing the latest, greatest buys?

In this atmosphere of rapidly declining worship attendance I have also heard people ask: Why do miracles seem to happen more often in other parts of the world than they happen here? It seems to me that devotion to worship (or lack thereof) and this apparent scarcity of miracles are related. Let me explain.

As mere human beings, we are greatly limited by our energies and attention spans. There is only so much we are able to focus on at once. On one hand, we are extremely fortunate to live in a wealthy, technologically advanced part of the world. We are seldom cold or dirty or hungry. Mostly, our houses are comfortably furnished, and when the temperature plunges to minus thirty-five, we don't particularly like it, but as the night wraps around we have our warm, soft beds to retreat to. Generally speaking, life is good here.

But that there's a spiritual downside to the good life. Because what we can absorb is limited by our senses, some of what would benefit our souls is left in the ditch beside a highway filled with a steady stream of bright, shining nothings that amuse us or boost self-esteem for a moment and then streak away. Miracles may be happening all along the roadside completely unnoticed and completely unmissed until someone asks the question: Where are the miracles?

Truth is, they're probably happening right here. But in other places devoted people, not as distracted by all the "comforts" as we are, may anticipate and welcome them when they arrive. Maybe all our comforts and deceiving glitter steal our attention from the miracles that would really change us.

Here in this land, where we have everything and want still more, no one's watching for a miracle, and few are praying for one in our church sanctuaries. Things are going too well for us to pay much attention to God. Perhaps there are a hundred miracles circling overhead like exhausted birds, just waiting and waiting for a place to land if only there were an open space and someone to notice.

The more we empty ourselves, the more room we give God to fill us.

— Mother Teresa

Don't Worry.
It's Not Your Job.

Luke 12:22–32

He said to his disciples, "That's why I tell you: Don't fret about life — what you're going to eat — or about your body — what you're going to wear. Remember, there is more to living than food and clothing. Think about the crows: they don't plant or harvest, they don't have storerooms or barns. Yet God feeds them. You're worth a lot more than the birds! Can any of you add an hour to life by fretting about it?"

I'm organized. Very organized indeed. Most of the time, this tendency is on my side. It helps prevent the bouts of worry that have plagued me since childhood.

What seems like a long time ago, when I was completing my student-teaching practicum in a rural Alberta school, I was encouraged to teach a Grade 9 social studies class as well as doing my regular assignment in a Grade 4 classroom. Foolishly and under a great deal of pressure, I agreed to take on the extra challenge.

One night as I lay in bed, my formerly sound organizational skills went crazy and turned on me. I had thoroughly planned the day to come, and everything that I could control was under control. I suppose my error was in reviewing just one more time my plans for the upcoming day. Then my mind, without my exhausted body's permission, moved onto attempting to organize those things over which I had no control. I wanted to accurately predict the kids' behaviour and moods and any unpleasant situations that might arise.

Of course, nothing short of a reliable crystal ball could solve my problem or assuage my worry. In response to all this crazy worry, my skin erupted into huge, itchy hives. At one o'clock in the morning I was in a hospital emergency ward looking like a bumpy toad while a kindly doctor fed me two antihistamines and told me to go home and get some sleep.

As I recall, the next day went fine. No one died or was seriously injured. And I never became a junior high school teacher.

Slowly I learned to limit my organization to those situations over which I have some control. Even though I still struggle not to worry about the things that I can't control, I understand that fretting doesn't add hours to my life. If it did, I'd be closing in on immortality!

Scripture tells us that it's not our responsibility to worry: it's a waste of valuable time and energy. And our spiritual devotion can get us off the "worry hook."

This reassurance that we don't need to worry leaves us with a question: What'll we do to fill all those hours we spend wringing our hands, getting migraine headaches, and breaking out in a million hives?

Perhaps thoughts of love and hope can fill our newly-vacant worry space. They're much friendlier tenants in the long run, and if we're lucky, these more helpful thoughts may eventually lead us to action. Just imagine a life in which no moments however brief are devoted to worry. Instead, this time is filled with action that helps to prevent or eliminate those problems that worry the world. Now that has the potential of adding an hour or two to someone's life.

Today is the tomorrow you worried about yesterday.
Was it worth it?

— Anonymous

Too Much Stuff

Mark 10:21–22

Jesus, looking at him, loved him and said, "You lack one thing; go, sell what you own, and give the money to the poor, and you will have treasure in heaven; then come, follow me." When he heard this, he was shocked and went away grieving, for he had many possessions.

---

*L*ately I've been thinking a lot about stuff. You see, this past weekend I was in the midst of moving my worldly belongings from one apartment to yet another. It's a positive move and signals good things to come for sure, but it reminds me once again how much stuff I haul around with me from life change to life change, moving slowly and agonizingly up and down endless flights of stairs, organizing and strategizing, renting vans and unhooking utilities. It reminds me that I simply have too much stuff.

Having moved three times in the course of seven months, I've considerably trimmed down what I own and lug around. Still, there are those things I just can't part with: the cat puppet Mom and Dad brought back for me from England in 1972, my grandma's heavy cooking pots, hard cover copies of my favourite novels, the bedroom suite that was the first my parents owned when they married in 1964. How do you let go of those things that remind you of who you are and where you've come from?

A wealthy young man comes to Jesus seeking advice. He has followed all the commandments and is a good, sincere guy who only wants to follow Christ. Recognizing this, Jesus instructs him that he has to do one more thing: get rid of all his stuff.

I often use this passage when I'm teaching young people. The students make a detailed list of all the things they own, they read the scripture, then on paper they give away and sell all their possessions so that they may follow Jesus. It starts out easy, parting with the items that don't mean much, but soon it gets tough. The gospel passage is often taken to imply that the young man leaves, unable to part with his belongings and choosing not to follow Jesus. I point out that the outcome is undetermined. Yes, the man goes away grieving, but he may be going away with the intention of parting with all he owns or at least considering what to do.

Who wouldn't grieve if presented with such a challenge? We're all attached to what we own. What I noticed today upon reading this familiar story again is the phrase, "Jesus, looking at him, loved him." Is it possible that Jesus gives the advice he does out of love? That he's not trying to construct obstacles this eager and devout fellow cannot possibly surmount? Perhaps Jesus is giving this man the gift of truth: "To follow me, you need to free yourself from the things that enslave you." Now this rich man is faced with a difficult decision, as we all are if we take this passage of scripture seriously.

If we see letting go of our material wealth as a gift, as a path to freedom to serve God, then it seems less like a sacrifice, more like something we can do to improve our spiritual selves. Of course, I doubt I'll ever part with my bedroom furniture or Grandma's cookware, but I'll try to clear my life of the kind of clutter that gets in the way of a relationship with my Creator.

Love and exclusive possession can never go together.

— Ghandi

God's Compass

Micah 7:7

But as for me, I will look to the Lord,
I will wait for the God of my salvation;
my God will hear me.

I thought it might happen sooner or later and now it has: I couldn't think of anything to write about for my newspaper column. Sure, I had missed submitting the occasional article but that was always because life suddenly became unexpectedly hectic and I just couldn't fit it in. But never before had I faced this big, blank space in my mind where an idea should be. It's a strange experience because often two ideas compete, and I'm forced to choose one. I transfer the other to a piece of scrap paper until I need it the next week or even later.

But this time there was nothing. Since I've been a faith columnist I've naturally depended on God to provide the inspiration to say something each week, and until this occasion it had always happened. Without fail, something that I considered worth saying would come to me.

It reminded me of other times in life when I didn't know which way to turn and I thought for sure that God was withholding direction for some reason unknown to me. I've spent a lot of time in those places, trying to think and pray and somehow stumble into moving forward again. It seems that God puts us into these apparently stagnant areas, where nothing seems clear and the outcome is fuzzy, to turn us around, to force us to consider where we are headed and whether it is the best destination for us.

We pray and we plead, "Dear God, give me the answer! Get me out of this going-nowhere place. I just want to be moving forward again."

Maybe that's the catch. Maybe God doesn't want us to travel forward in the same course any more. Maybe we're intended instead to scoot off to one side or even take a few confident steps straight backwards. Or possibly we are just supposed to sit still and find our bearings instead of plunging blindly ahead into the unknown.

That's where I am today: sitting here still as can be with no ahead in sight and no way to move much in any direction. But I know it's going to be okay. It always is. The evidence is right in front of me. I feared that God was denying me a topic for that week's column, but here it is as if it had been there all along, just waiting for me to capture the words and turn them into readable ink-stains.

If you can find a path with no obstacles, it probably doesn't lead anywhere.

— Frank A. Clark

Reflections On Special Times

Death Before Rebirth
(*Lent and Passiontide*)

Isaiah 26:19

Your dead shall live, their
corpses shall rise.
O dwellers in the dust, awake
and sing for joy!
For your dew is a radiant dew,
and the earth will give birth to
those long dead.

---

*A*h. Easter. Brightly-coloured straw baskets filled with milk choco late eggs line the store shelves to tempt me as I grocery shop for more nutritionally balanced items. Daffodils and daisies look out of place in the florist's department as snow falls just outside those big glass doors and consumers struggle with car keys, lists, and shopping carts. Hot cross buns, stuffed bunnies, and fuzzy chicks point us forward to this season that hails spring and renewed optimism.

But it's still the season of Passiontide. The stories it tells are of anguish, betrayal, and torture. It is about death and mourning and waiting in the dark for the sun to rise.

No wonder our focus strays to cream-filled eggs and white choco late rabbits and baby animals — the pleasant, light stuff of commercialized Easter — that appears in the stores sometimes weeks before the season of Lent even commences. But how can we antici pate rebirth without first feeling a part of ourselves die, and how can we celebrate the triumph over pain without having first ached? Hearts can't be mended without first being broken, and no one can be resur rected before experiencing the chill of death.

Do we expect spring to follow autumn in this winter land of

ours? No. (It would be nice, but ....) It's the same with Easter. Getting there requires passing through the valley of the shadow of death.

I know. It is tempting to leap right into the celebration of life. And I'm all for celebrating! In this feel-good society where quick fixes and individual happiness are top priority, it's sometimes difficult to see why we should mourn again a death that's been died, cry again tears that have been cried, utter prayers again that have been prayed. If remembering is painful, why do it?

Because (I'll say it again — it bears repeating) without death, there can be no rebirth and that rebirth is Easter. That's the point. That's the whole idea behind flowers, baby bunnies, Easter eggs and newly-hatched chicks. They're symbols of life, evidence that life somehow conquers death and light floods the darkness.

No death, no miracle and hence, no Easter. I'm not suggesting that you need to weep bitterly for weeks on end, but I am suggesting some quiet time to contemplate the meaning of Lent. With this done, the chocolate will seem sweeter, the eggs more colourful, and the gift of life more miraculous.

A miracle is an event which creates faith. That is the purpose and nature of miracles. Frauds deceive. An event which creates faith does not deceive: therefore it is not a fraud, but a miracle.

— George Bernard Shaw

Love Remains the Greatest
(*Easter*)

Luke 23:33–34

When they came to the place that is called The Skull, they crucified Jesus there with the criminals, one on his right and one on his left. Then Jesus said, "Father, forgive them; for they do not know what they are doing."

—

A long time ago when I was attending university, an education professor blasted me for handing in a test paper directly to him instead of placing it on his desk. It was a small, nearly microscopic incident in the span of my lifetime, but it still makes me angry when I think about it. And I think about it surprisingly often. The guy was really just a power-tripper and I should let it go. Yet I don't.

It's not that I'm a particularly petty person. (At least I don't think so — it's difficult to be objective about some things, especially subjective things.) I think I'm probably pretty much the same as most people. There are actions and folks who are difficult to forgive, and memory keeps us holding on tight to our grudges as if they could buoy us up in a flood. Truth is, they're more like rocks in our pockets. Still, we fill our pockets to bulging as the water rises.

That's why this gospel passage is so wondrous. How beyond our understanding is this type of forgiveness. It doesn't seem possible to forgive someone who is torturing you to death and gambling over the clothing they stripped from your body moments ago. Yet it was possible. It was possible for Jesus to forgive his torturers.

And I can't let go of some old professor's snide comment. The man's likely dead by now, and still I allow my stubbornness to keep me from the freedom of forgiveness. Talk about perspective!

Throughout the gospels, Jesus' most prominent message to his followers is to love everyone, including our enemies. That message is essential to understanding who Jesus was and what he stood for. That was his radical, life-altering, healing belief: that love could overcome illness, oppression, hatred, violence, and even death. Indeed it was love that restored life to Lazarus, it was love that accepted tax-collectors and women as friends, it was love that healed the lepers' open wounds and mended people's broken hearts.

But never was Jesus' message made so clear as it was that day atop Golgotha where anyone outwardly rejecting Roman authority paid a severe price for their political or religious rebellion. For days they hung, bound and nailed, at the mercy of scavenger fowl, wild dogs, the heat of the day and cold of the night, and of their own wracked bodies, to serve as an example to anyone else who would defy Roman law. Somehow he stood by his message of love, forgiving from the height of the torture device constructed to kill him slowly.

Certainly, the empty tomb and the resurrection of Christ are symbols and events full of hope and evidence of what faith can do. But perhaps the most crucial point is the forgiveness from the cross. Isn't that love in action conquering the dark of violent death by simply appearing where not expected? Without the love, without the forgiveness, without the compassion at his death, would the story of Jesus' resurrection bring the same joy?

I've lived so long with this story that it's hard to picture, but I believe the messages of faith and hope found in that empty tomb and on the road to Emmaus come second. Death was beaten first on the cross by Jesus' words of forgiveness before he died and conquered again in his rising.

Forgiveness does not change the past,
but it does enlarge the future.

— Paul Boese

Everyone Rise
(*Easter*)

Isaiah 26:19

O dwellers in the dust, awake and sing for joy!

———

*L*ast winter I gave up my home downtown and moved to the suburbs. It's different all right, but it's nice enough. One of the nice things is the flowerbed that runs the length of the west side of the house where I live. Until yesterday, that narrow strip of dirt was a tangle of dead brown stalks, their once-green leaves shrivelled and dry. Several days ago, I noticed first one spike of life piercing the dead jungle, reaching for the sun, then another. I looked closer and spotted many more light-seeking shoots poking up through the soil beneath the clutter of last year's garden.

So yesterday afternoon with the sun warm on my back, I knelt on the concrete sidewalk and took ten minutes out of my day to free the new life from the dead. When I had pulled the old dead clutter away, I smoothed the soil with my hands, set down a large plaster bumblebee, and poked a wooden red tulip into a place where there was no real plant life. Today I'll go buy some flower seeds, thereby doing my bit to encourage life and colour in this season of spring.

It's no coincidence that we celebrate our Christian holiday of resurrection and new life at the onset of spring when there are symbols of new life all around in expected and unexpected places alike. The new plants remind me that flowerbeds are not the only things on this earth with the ability to experience resurrection, death, and rebirth into new life.

One day, a heavy man visits his doctor and discovers he has dangerously high blood pressure. On his way home, he stops in at Zellers and purchases a treadmill. Now every day he watches the early news and drinks 500 mls of water while he walks. His health steadily improves and by May, he's out running in the park with his son-in-law.

On that same day, a wife wakes to find that her husband didn't come home the night before. Within an hour, she receives a phone call from him. He's fine, so don't worry. In fact, he's better than he's ever been. He's fallen in love with someone else. Should've told her sooner, he admits, but he's telling her now. His lawyer will be in touch and he promises to be fair. This isn't her fault.

She cries, lying in a trembling heap on the linoleum by the fridge. Around seven o'clock that evening, she rises, makes herself a cup of tea and checks her e-mail. Then she showers and goes to bed early, gulping three or four tablespoons of cough syrup to knock her out. The next day, she colours her hair for the first time in ten years. She paints her nails, too. Red. By that afternoon, she's enrolled in a pottery class. Why not?

Miracles happen every day. Souls die and are brought back to life through hope granted by the Creator. Easter isn't the only appropriate time to celebrate resurrection, but it's a wonderful reminder of its power and of the gift of new life granted us all.

The very least you can do in your life is to figure out what you hope for. And the most you can do is live inside that hope. Not admire it from a distance but live right in it, under its roof.

— Barbara Kingsolver

To Wait Is Holy
(*Advent*)

Isaiah 30:18

Blessed are all they that wait for Him.

I'm waiting for a new guitar. You see, I have a guitar, an old one that used to belong to my grandfather, but it's not a very good guitar and it's quite difficult to play. There's way too much space between the strings and fret board, and that makes it really hard for me to correctly depress the strings with my tiny fingers. When I began my lessons a few months ago, I promised myself that when I could play a variety of scales and a little music, I would be allowed to buy a new instrument. That kind of incentive made it easier to wait for what I want.

But now my music teacher says that I would progress much more quickly if I had a new guitar. She's strongly encouraging me to consider getting a new acoustic sooner, and she lets me play her old, solid Gibson to show me what a difference an excellent instrument makes. All of a sudden, it's harder to be patient. I want that brand-new guitar now!

In this instant society of ours, most of us hate waiting. We don't like sitting at the flashing red lights, waiting for that impossibly long train to inch its way past. Some of us sit at our desks glancing every few minutes at that blank white face telling us that soon we'll be free from one chore to dash onto the next, from meeting to meeting, homework page to hockey practice, exercise class to pottery. Others of us, owners of computers from the Jurassic period, sit in our swivel chairs and spin while ages pass as an entire colour photograph is downloaded.

Events move quickly in our world and, as much as this fact causes us a measure of stress and anxiety, for many of us it's what we've grown used to. Hectic is now our comfort zone. Not that we're comfortable there, but it's what we've grown to believe life should be. Dashing from here to there and back again may not bring us peace, but it's at least familiar. So we do it without thinking much about why, and we feel unease when there's unexpected waiting time in between our bursts of sprinting.

The season of Advent challenges us to slow down and to engage consciously in that thing we most dislike — waiting. How do we do this in our rush-rush world where adrenaline is the drink of gods and wasting time is a mortal sin? How do we go against the flow of things in order to honour the time before the Saviour's arrival?

I suppose there's no easy solution, and how we find and use a quiet time is up to each us to decide. Some of us may pray the rosary each day while others may light a candle within a wreath to remember. Perhaps some folks add to their bathroom reading or bedside tables an Advent devotion to help focus attention, even just for moments, on the season at hand. One positive aspect of our instant society is that it's currently bursting with quick, accessible spiritual resources and some of these could definitely aid us in our wait for the Christ child. It doesn't particularly matter what works for each person as long as we make the effort to seek it out.

As my guitar practice requires devotion and concentration, so does our wait for Jesus' arrival. It's the wait that magnifies the holiness of the event.

—⋯—

Nothing great is created suddenly, any more than a bunch of grapes or a fig. If you tell me that you desire a fig. I answer you that there must be time. Let it first blossom, then bear fruit, then ripen.

— Epictetus

The Greatest Love Of All
(*Valentine's Day*)

Matthew 22:36–39

"Teacher, which commandment in the law is the greatest?"
Jesus said to him, "'You shall love the Lord your God with
all your heart, all your soul, and with all your mind.'" This is
the greatest and first commandment. And a second is like it:
'You shall love your neighbour as yourself.' "

---

*I*t's Valentine's Day, but I don't want to write about smoochy, lovey-dovey, card-selling love — the kind of love that compels a man to make reservations at a nice restaurant and a woman to wear undergarments about as comfortable as a mild case of shingles. I want to tackle a more difficult topic — compassion. It would be easier for me to talk about romance, how we make our partners' lives easier, how those sweet, little gestures help get us through the day to day. Compassion is much larger. It's huge. It's a responsibility, a way of life, a way of perceiving every person and every situation. That's the love I want to talk about.

Where to begin? Well, just this morning I heard an interview with Stephen Lewis, the United Nations' special envoy for the HIV and AIDS pandemic in Africa. He spoke of the resilience of the continent's people, their struggles and hopes, their sufferings and deaths. Not long ago, he toured a hospital where every fifteen minutes, AIDS takes the life of another child. He told of the tiny aluminum coffins that the staff wheel right into the dorms to transfer those young bodies from bed to eternal rest. Right there on the radio, he cried. Many of these people had become his friends. That's what compassion does.

Compassion's not easy. It means loving everyone as you love yourself. It's a tall order — feeling their pain as your own, their illnesses and mourning as sharply as if your own body or your own heart were breaking. It also means sharing in their joy, in their triumphs and successes, in their view of life. Compassion may sometimes hurt, but nothing else can open you up to others the way it can if you allow it to do so.

It's a life-altering decision to love your neighbour as you love yourself, to see everyone through compassionate eyes. I struggle with it on and off, always a little afraid because big change is frightening. Sometimes, little by little, I find myself edging tentatively closer to feeling a deep, general compassion. At times, such as hearing Stephen Lewis speak of the horrendous events he's witnessed, I admire his compassion, wish I could be that loving. But then I withdraw. Compassion gives power and meaning to words, bestows on words a life force, and images like those that Stephen Lewis paints in words hurt when heard with an open heart.

Maybe that's what compassion can do for people. It can give us power and meaning, bestow a life force on the words we say and hear. To me, that's bigger than any love represented by a bouquet of roses or box of chocolates.

———

What does love look like? It has the hands to help others. It has the feet to hasten to the poor and needy. It has eyes to see misery and want. It has the ears to hear the sighs and sorrows of men. That is what love looks like.

— St. Augustine

The Song of Solomon: A Love Story (*Valentine's Day*)

The Song of Solomon 8:6

Set me as a seal upon your heart,
as a seal upon your arm,
for love is strong as death,
passion fierce as the grave.
Its flashes are flashes of fire,
a raging flame.

———

*T*here is a book in the Bible I like to read aloud to my friends. It leaves them with hearts pounding, wide-eyed, dry-mouthed, and barely able to stammer, "*That's* in the Bible?"

Yes, indeed, folks. It's in the Bible. In the particular Bible that lies open before me right now, it is a mere sex — oh, pardon me — *six* pages long. So it's a nice, short read that holds some of the most beautiful, passionate love poetry I've ever encountered.

With Valentine's Day nearly upon us, I thought it appropriate to write about this book that features two young lovers sharing their romantic feelings for each other. It's obviously not Platonic friendship these young people are going on and on about. Oh sure, the scholars have debated, arguing back and forth:

"It's an allegory that speaks of God's love for Israel!"

"Oh no, it's not! Clearly it represents Christ's love for the church!"

This debate is fine by me because I have these "religious allegory" arguments to thank for the inclusion of this compelling, somewhat steamy bit of writing in the Old Testament of my Christian Bible. The majority of biblical scholars now pretty much agree that *The Song of Solomon* is about love with all its physical desire and yearning.

And why shouldn't an entire book of the Bible be devoted to celebrating the miracle of romantic love? After all, the Bible celebrates the beauty of creation, the miracle of God's love for humankind and of people for one another in a non-romantic context. Why should it not celebrate sweet physical attraction, the miracle of finding one person whom you desire above all others? Isn't this feeling of love another wonderful gift God has bestowed upon us, and isn't it one role of scripture to make us aware of such blessings?

The Song of Solomon tells the story of a young couple anticipating physical love. I specify that they're "anticipating" love because, as the story goes, they are engaged to be married and have not yet shared any physical love. In the verses, they speak directly to one another and to friends regarding their feelings.

I like *The Song of Solomon* because it explores a universal theme. It helps me to more easily relate to the colourful characters presented in stories throughout the Bible. It lets me know that basic emotions and needs have remained the same throughout the centuries. To understand that although hundreds of years separate us, people in biblical times were lonely, afraid, falling in love and experiencing joy, grief, and worry, makes Bible stories seem more present, more real to me.

For our wedding ceremonies, I believe that we should keep our traditional marriage passages from John and Genesis regarding the creation of and the sacred union between a man and a woman. But when the wedding's through, the cake's been eaten, and the guests have gone home, don't forget to slip a copy of *The Song of Solomon* into your luggage before you set out on your honeymoon!

'Tis said of love that it sometimes goes, sometimes flies; runs with one, walks gravely with another; turns a third into ice, and sets a fourth in a flame: it wounds one, another it kills: like lightning it begins and ends in the same moment: it makes that fort yield at night which it besieged but in the morning; for there is no force able to resist it.

— Miguel De Cervantes

The Ties That Bind
(*Thanksgiving*)

Psalm 69:30

I will praise the name of God with a song;
I will magnify him with thanksgiving.

———

This Thanksgiving weekend I'll be driving a long stretch of high-way. It's not the roasted turkey or the cranberry sauce, the pump-kin pie or the mashed potatoes that will compel me to travel those miles and miles through Alberta's consistently inconsistent October weather. It's the family who wait at the other end of the road, the people I haven't seen in more than a year, and the memories and stories held in the intricate web of the family to which I also belong.

I used to feel a little cynical about family holidays. The unrealis-tic way they're portrayed in sitcoms and old movies — the chain of hysterical antics performed by scrubbed-clean children with immov-able hair — kind of jaded me, I suppose. Holidays never seemed so neat and tidy in my world or in the worlds of my closest friends, and even at a young age, I understood that to expect them to be perfect was unrealistic. Yet I have to admit feeling some disappointment when they weren't all warm and fuzzy. But who doesn't?

Now I'm older and perhaps slightly wiser. Suddenly, there seems to be more value in those snow-too-early, cream-corn-burned-to-the-bottom-of-the-pot, and the-relatives-are-crazy Thanksgivings than in the picture-perfect ones I never really believed in. I understand now that three-dimensional lives necessarily have more life and more layers than a magazine picture of a perfect family created from a mould.

Like a kitchen that's cooked in, visited in, and celebrated in, a life that's thoroughly lived gets a little messy at times. Those some-times untidy and unruly holidays when things don't go as smoothly as we would wish are evidence of real living and of our humanness. Mortal people don't always get along, turkeys aren't always perfectly browned, and inevitably there's going to be at least one person at the table who hasn't yet developed a taste for Grandma's extra-tart homemade cranberry sauce.

With time and experience I now understand that any close group of people, family or friends or a combination of the two, are going to experience friction, disappointments, even tragedies. I've also learned that these things can be mostly overcome or adapted to through love and forgiveness.

Sound simple? Yeah, right. It's very difficult, but it's not impossible because I witness it all the time. People keep coming together season after season even though they have good reasons for never getting together again. Hurtful and unpleasant things happen in life and between folks. But I have seen love and forgiveness keep together relationships that are fragile, frayed, but very necessary. After a while, and with much persistence, they have regained strength and stamina and continue to provide a nurturing place for memories and a shared history to develop and grow.

So I will drive those miles (on clear highways, I hope) and meet with the people who have forgiven and accepted me all along and still welcome me back into the web that joins us. Life doesn't guarantee that it will be a perfect Thanksgiving, but that's not exactly what I'm wanting. What I want is a real Thanksgiving — complete with real people, real memories, and real good food.

Gratitude unlocks the fullness of life. It turns what we have into enough, and more. It turns denial into acceptance, chaos to order, confusion to clarity. It can turn a meal into a feast, a house into a home, a stranger into a friend. Gratitude makes sense of our past, brings peace for today, and creates a vision for tomorrow.

— Melody Beattie

Dress Up As Yourself
(*Hallowe'en*)

Psalm 139:11–12

If I say, "Surely the darkness
shall cover me,
and the light around me
become night,"
even the darkness is not dark
to you;
the night is as bright as
the day,
for darkness is as light to you.

$\mathcal{T}$he other evening I was out celebrating Hallowe'en with a group
of friends.It was still pretty early as we sat there enjoying each
other's company and admiring the costumes. There were the usual
ghosts and ghouls, superheroes and sailors, cowboys and Careys (Drew
Careys, that is). There were a couple of Q-tips accompanied by a
very pretty ear, a Spiderman, a whole ensemble of Ghost Busters, the
entire cast of the musical *Grease*, and one or two Zorros.

My chair faced the dance floor and from there I noticed that
despite the relatively early hour, people were out there dancing and
mingling in a way that doesn't usually happen until long after midnight. People looked right at one another and smiled. In the kind of
setting where often people greet one another with suspicion and side-
ways glances, spoken and unspoken compliments were being passed
around like hors d'oeuvres

So what was the difference that evening? The setting was essentially
the same, although adorned with a few orange and black streamers
and balloons, and many of the clientele probably frequented this
spot on weekends yet didn't necessarily behave in this friendlier, freer

manner. If it wasn't the setting and wasn't the people, I figured that it had to be the costumes.

What's with costumes? I think it has to do directly with *not* being ourselves, with being somebody or something else for just one night. You see, when we lose the self, we lose the self-consciousness and some of the barriers to human contact that we erect for ourselves.

If I'm right that we feel better and less inhibited when we are not ourselves, what is it about ourselves that makes us ashamed or shy or overly cautious about revealing who we are? Why is there release in hiding, in pretending we are someone else?

I picture it this way. Each of us knows our innermost workings in a way that no other person can or ever will. We see each physical and emotional scar from the inside out. We have a front row seat at a private show each time our failures, poor choices, or wrongdoings prance across our mind's eye in larger than life colour, taunting us and reminding us of their existence.

So we hide. We cannot allow what is on the inside to be put on display and so choose instead to shroud it in darkness. But God knows what's there. And, it would appear, God loves us still!

Is it possible that we are created with the potential for flaws rather than with the potential for perfection because God delights in our discovery of ourselves and in our learning and growth? In the scriptures we are reassured that we are valuable in God's eyes — not as someone else but as our truest selves, the whole package. God has forgiven us, so perhaps it's time to forgive ourselves, to call a recess in the eternal trial.

Let's put ourselves at rest and give ourselves permission to let go of some of the weight that's breaking our spiritual backs. But surprise! Letting go will feel like putting on a Hallowe'en costume. Better still, it will feel like being born into a new skin, only it will be the best skin, our own real skin that we will not have to take off before we go to bed!

—

Accept everything about yourself — I mean everything.
You are you and that is the
beginning and the end — no apologies, no regrets.

— Clark Moustakas

The Mall Won't Miss You
(*The Christmas Season*)

Ecclesiastes 5:18–20

This is what I have seen to be good: it is fitting to eat and
drink and find enjoyment in all the toil with which one toils
under the sun the few days of the life God gives us;
for this is our lot. Likewise all to whom God gives wealth
and possessions and whom he enables to enjoy them, and to
accept their lot and find enjoyment in their toil —
this is the Gift of God. For they will scarcely brood over
the days of their lives because God keeps them occupied
with the joy of their hearts.

---

*T*he evidence of wealth lies all around us this shopping season.
Debit and credit cards flash beneath the department store lights
like so many winter stars while too many delectable items to mention line the store shelves and overflow into the aisles. People stalk up
and down in search of just the right gifts. Some emerge triumphant,
satisfied with their purchases, and some search in vain.

I rarely feel satisfied after any shopping experience, even when
I'm shopping for myself. Most often I end up feeling inadequate —
either under-dressed or out of style or just plain old too poor. But
miraculously, when I leave the shops and get back to life, my feelings
of inadequacy vanish. I no longer feel that my self-esteem is under
attack or that I need those new shoes to feel fulfilled, which is how I
can feel when confronted with merchandise in a store setting.

There is so much pressure to buy, especially at this time of year,
that it is easy to overlook and enjoy those riches that we already possess. The pressure to purchase leaves me feeling empty and hungry
when in reality I'm stuffed. That's the problem.

My craving for more doesn't allow me to enjoy all of the gifts that God has granted me. Instead of being occupied with the joy of my heart, I find myself occupied with budgeting, with dredging up fresh ideas for what to buy, with feeling that what I buy can never be enough and that who I am I can never be enough no matter what I buy.

Perhaps my problem lies in not enjoying enough. In my pursuit of things I believe will eventually make me happy, I neglect taking the time to be happy for what I have. Constantly wanting more makes us feel that we are lacking something and robs us of opportunities to feel grateful and therefore wealthy. In the end, the things that we seek out in order to fill our hearts with joy may be responsible for making our hearts feel empty.

The good news is that, according to the author of Ecclesiastes, we have a responsibility to notice and savour all the delicious things that we've been given. Our enjoyment need not be selfish. One way to enjoy what we possess is to share our abundance with others. This can also leave us feeling wealthier yet, and may even fill some of those heart-gaps left by the consumer experience.

So go ahead this holiday season and take the gifts God has given you. Take five whole minutes to let one chocolate melt on your tongue. Build a snowman with your kids. Lie on your picnic table one clear night and pick out the constellations.

The stores won't miss you — they're full enough already — and your heart may thank you.

Both abundance and lack exist simultaneously in our lives, as parallel realities. It is always our conscious choice which secret garden we will tend … when we choose not to focus on what is missing from our lives but are grateful for the abundance that's present — love, health, family, friends, work, the joys of nature and personal pursuits that bring us pleasure — the wasteland of illusion falls away and we experience Heaven on earth.

— Sarah Ban Breathnach

Amid the Flashing Of Forks
(*Christmas*)

Ecclesiastes 2:24

There is nothing better for mortals than to eat and
drink, and find enjoyment in their toil.

---

*M*om began cooking on Christmas Eve. While we were hanging
our stockings and shaking and prodding the gifts beneath the
tree, she was in the kitchen preparing the stuffing, baking cookies,
and slicing up vegetables.

Before the presents were all open and the first pot of coffee was
empty, she was back in the kitchen, plopping the huge turkey into a
roaster, sliding it into the oven, and arranging pots on the stovetop.
All morning the house gradually warmed and sweet smells slowly
permeated the air as the food simmered and stewed. We all waited
with anticipation, stealing a pickle here, a shortbread cookie there,
waiting and waiting for the call, "Dinner time!"

About mid-afternoon, following the arrival of the grandparents
and an aunt and an uncle, the call finally came. We weren't far away
— just hovering around in the living room on the other side of the
wall. At the sound of Mom's voice, we leapt off the couch as quickly
as if we'd just noticed it was on fire.

The family sat down together, Dad directing traffic and everyone else commenting on how wonderful everything looked. The pale
glow from the flames of red candles in the centre of the table made
the crystal glasses sparkle like winter stars. China bowls heaped with
every culinary delight steamed beneath our noses, and dishes brought
out once a year flaunted their shine. We took it all in briefly before
saying grace and whispering a solemn "Amen."

Then, every year, in the course of twelve and a half minutes, we
inhaled that entire meal. Amid the gnashing of teeth and the flashing

of forks, the turkey and mashed potatoes disappeared faster than Frosty in July. The pickles and cranberry sauce soon became bitter and sweet memories, and the dessert waiting and watching from the countertop shivered at its fate.

With a belch from Grandpa and a withering look from Grandma, it was done. The feast that had taken a day and a half to prepare had been eaten in less time than it would take to load the dishwasher.

It makes me think of our approach to Christmas, to the Christmas story in particular, and of the symbols we use to retell the story. I love these symbols, especially the manger scene complete with Mary, Joseph, the sheep and cows, a couple of shepherds, and always three wise men bearing three gifts. At the centre of attention, lying in a trough, is the newborn Jesus. It's beautiful and serene and able evoke that Christmas feeling when nothing else seems able to draw it out.

But haven't we arrived at the ending? Did we gulp down the whole story without pausing to savour the individual elements and flavours of the tale?

Do we stop to enjoy that which has been carefully prepared and laid out before us both to nourish us and bring us joy, or do we wolf it down in one fell swoop, knowing it's good but not taking the time to really taste it?

When I was a little kid, I set up the Christmas scene with a plastic cow and Mary and Joseph staring adoringly at the matchbox I had filled with imitation straw. It wasn't until late on Christmas Eve that I used to put Jesus into the manger. Maybe that little girl, savouring the story piece by piece, had the right idea.

I asked God for all things, that I might enjoy life. God gave life, that I might enjoy all things.

— Source unknown

Resolving Not To Resolve
(*New Year's*)

Ecclesiastes 7:15–18

In my vain life I have seen everything; there are
righteous people who perish in their righteousness, and
there are wicked people who prolong their life in their
evildoing. Do not be too righteous, and do not act too wise;
why should you destroy yourself? Do not be too wicked,
and do not be a fool; why should you die before your time?
It is good that you should take hold of the one, without
letting go of the other; for the one who fears God shall
succeed with both.

I haven't seen them yet but I know they're coming. You know what
I'm talking about: those ads on television, radio, and public bul-
letin boards telling you that now is the time to change those things
you dislike about yourself, time to unveil the new you. Conveniently,
these ad writers know exactly the "new you" you should unveil — in
case you didn't know what you were supposed to find under that
white starched cloth when it was finally ceremonially lifted.

So they tell us. Ladies, you know what's most important — the
crowds at the gym in January will attest to it. Yes, we must be thin-
ner. Skinnier is happier. While you're becoming trim, you also need
to get a computer (if you haven't already got one) and learn how to use it,
colour your hair, buy new clothes, and replace all your cosmetics. You
must strive to contentedly manage family and work simultaneously, not
for a moment begrudging either. Then, finally, you will be perfect and
worthy of being put on display. Until next season.

And guys, the advertisers have spotted you with all your cash in the bank. You've become prime targets. Did you know that none of you are having enough sex and there are several brand-spanking-new solutions to remedy your receding hairline? Now you have a use for the money gathering dust and interest, and there are new and better investment opportunities to increase it. Now you can buy happiness What? You thought you were happy fishing with your grandkids, riding your bike, watching Monday night football with a buddy, or walking with your wife? Well, apparently you were wrong.

Sigh. If only there were an easier, less expensive way to be happy. Perfection seems like such a steep goal. I turned to Ecclesiastes (probably my most favourite book) in hopes of a solution different from the ones offered by the folks who benefit from us purchasing their products. There I found the above verse. It seems a little cynical on the surface, but I think it has something to offer in the way of a mini-lesson on self-acceptance.

"Take the good with the bad. God's given you a many-faceted personality. Trust God and you will do well with those sometimes contradictory elements" is how I interpret it. If I'm right (even partly right), it sounds like advice worth taking.

Happiness seems to be more attainable through acceptance of self and others than through making prescribed changes. Maybe in the long run it's more worthwhile to resolve to accept than to resolve to change some surface things. Of course, if you are engaging in behaviour obviously destructive to self and others, change is necessary. But those extra ten pounds and the bald spot aren't killing anyone, and the world's not going to tip off its orbit if you don't get those new slacks or the girl who looks like she's straight out of a beer commercial.

So I propose that we resolve not to resolve this year — unless it's to resolve to accept that we are not perfect. Embrace your little imperfections. They're a part of you. Please don't discard them so easily. They may even be what make you extra lovable to someone! Now that's something to celebrate on New Year's Eve!

———

When you aim for perfection, you discover it's a moving target.

— Geoffrey F. Fisher

A Suitcase Of Sorrow
(New Year's)

Job 38:4

Where were you when I laid the foundations of the earth?

---

*Y*ou know how some people react to birthdays. They become blue or downright irritable upon pondering the passing of time, the fading of youth. Some are visibly uncomfortable when attention is focused on their special day, and some put on a brave front and silently grit their teeth when the cake and gifts appear or when they wake to forty pink flamingos gracing the front lawn.

New Year's always causes me the same kind of angst that birthdays cause these folks. I've never been a big fan of New Year's celebrations. It's not that I don't understand why it's supposed to be a happy time. The dawning of a new year symbolizes a fresh start, a clean slate, another chance to be who we would be and do what we would do. The future holds hope.

I get it. But my problem doesn't lie with the future. The past is my big stumbling block. At New Year's I take stock of all my failures, of all the disappointments, of all the mistakes I've made. As the clock nears midnight, my anxiety grows while through my mind run pictures of all the time I've wasted and of all the energy I've expended on fruitless endeavours.

You would think that the clock striking midnight would finally release me from the clutches of the past into the forgiving hands of the future. You'd think that with the first sip of champagne I'd be able to move on. But no. Every negative emotion and each sad memory is carefully strung on the cord like a broken Christmas light and the whole thing is stubbornly dragged across the border that divides the past from the future. After all the New Years I've seen, I still don't know why I do this. Could it be that, though my mistakes, downfalls, and regrets are a heavy and unpleasant burden, they're at least familiar and safe and I'm afraid to leave them behind? Maybe they are the anchor that gives me permission to stay where I am, to not try as hard, to not bother using up any more energy in the attempt to make life-improving changes.

I think this year I'll leave some of my baggage behind. I won't promise to leave it all, but I'll leave as much as I'm able. A suitcase of sorrow, a filing cabinet of grudges and broken friendships, a trunk or two of self-doubt and disappointments. To help ensure that a lot of the stuff that's pulling me down actually gets left in the past, I plan to destroy symbols of my troubles before the clock strikes twelve.

Then instead of putting my emphasis on the future, perhaps I'll try to set my focus on the moment I'm in. There's nothing I can do to change the past and I can control very little of what lies ahead. It'll be best to let both of them go.

When I lift my glass this evening, it will be neither to the future nor to the past, but only to the present where I actually live.

———

The secret of health for both mind and body is not to mourn for the past, not to worry about the future, or not to anticipate troubles, but to live in the present moment wisely and earnestly.

— The Buddha

The Anticlimactic
Potato Ricer
(*Mother's Day*)

Mark 3:31–35

Then his mother and his brothers came; and standing
outside, they sent to him and called. A crowd was sitting
around him; and they said to him, "Your mother and your
brothers and sisters are outside, asking for you." And he
replied, "Who are my mother and my brothers?" And
looking at those who sat around him, he said, "Here are my
mother and my brothers! Whoever does the will of God is
my brother and sister and mother."

---

*W*hen I was ten or eleven years old, my Dad gave me $10 and
sent me off to small-town downtown to purchase a gift for Mom
for Mother's Day that upcoming Sunday. I wandered from store to
store, eyeing little glass trinkets, teacups and saucers, cheap jewelry
and cheaper cologne, but the thing I discovered that most held my
attention was a larger-than-life glossy poster of Shaun Cassidy wearing a satin jacket. Oh, how I loved Shaun Cassidy!

After much deliberation and soul-searching, I decided that I
would buy that poster and hang it in my room. After all, Dad was
surely going to buy Mom a nice present, kind of a blanket family
gift. As long as my name was on the card, I'd be relieved of the responsibility of present finding. So what was the big deal?

When I arrived home with my poster, my father let me know
exactly. I had been selfish. The money and the time I spent shopping
were intended to produce a thoughtful gift for my only mother for the
only day dedicated solely to mothers. The "big deal" was Mother's Day.

My dad and I immediately hopped in the car, drove back downtown, and purchased a potato ricer for my mother. Yes, a potato ricer. I apologize for the anticlimactic ending, but this ain't fiction, folks, and mostly reality's just not that romantic.

It is easy to overlook the small things we do that unintentionally hurt our mothers. I don't believe that Jesus' purpose in the above passage was to hurt his mother or his siblings, but imagine how Mary must have felt hearing her son ask, "Who are my mother and my brothers?"

Probably she wouldn't have thought right off, "Why, what a clever point my son is making regarding the universality of God's family."

I think she would have felt disregarded and let down. If Mary heard Jesus' words , she would have been hurt. Any mother would.

Mothers sacrifice much to have and raise children. I realize that many blessings are incurred through becoming a parent, but I have seen what mothers have to give and it's tons: tons of affection, patience, time, discipline, strategy, organization, and work. Mary gave her all — all her love, devotion, and faith. And what heartache it nearly ended in!

But what blessing, too! Mary was chosen as the mother of God's only son, the Saviour. She understood well the honour of being Jesus' mother. At the same time she realized the risk she took in having that child. The baby might grow to be famous and loved, but he might also die a tragic death. It's a risk every mother takes.

So imagine the pain Jesus' words might have caused his mother. I wonder if she mentioned it to him. Or did she recognize his intention?

My intention in purchasing that Shaun Cassidy poster was certainly not to hurt my mother, but had I not recognized her special day in some small way, she probably would've been a little hurt. Fortunately for me, I was able to redeem myself through the presentation of a potato ricer and receive a really big hug that Sunday morning.

Motherhood is the strangest thing, it can be like being one's own Trojan horse.

— Rebecca West

Not Quite Out Of Time
(*Birthdays*)

Psalm 90:9–10

For all our days pass away under
your wrath;
our years come to an end like
a sigh.
The days of our life are seventy
years,
or perhaps eighty, if we are
strong;
even then their span is only toil
and trouble;
they are soon gone, and we fly
away.

———

Birthdays. What can be said? Well, let me try to say something. My birthday is bearing down upon me quickly and, like other maturing adults, I guess I'm not quite where'd I'd like to be yet. I wish time would grant me a little leeway, maybe slowing down just a tad so my life goals could catch up, but I've a sneaking suspicion I'm out of luck, if not quite out of time.

Remember when you used to count the days until your birthday, wishing the hours would evaporate like water droplets on a hot griddle? And now you sit amazed as the day approaches faster than a steam train on greased rails and wonder, "Where does the time go?" and "Can I leap out of the way before this birthday flattens another year?"

It doesn't seem possible that you could be this age already. After all, you can remember your own father at this age and he was an old guy! So what does that make you? What does it make your dad now, out there in his garden nurturing his tomato plants or swimming lengths at the crack of dawn in the local pool at his impossibly old age?

Although time has changed your body, you feel like the same person on the inside. Well, mostly. Your heart has a scar or two where it mended, and it's never been quite perfect and trusting since. Your memory bank is fuller than it's ever been, and the sadder memories always seem to be elbowing aside the pleasant, calming ones. Some days you keep them at bay; some days they find their way into your conscious thoughts.

If someone asked you to recount those birthday parties you once waited for with nearly painful anticipation, they'd be nothing but a colourful blur of paper hats, frosted cakes, and unnamable presents and guests. Sure, a few birthday moments stand out. Like the time your well-meaning mom put money in the cake and little Laura chipped her tooth on a dime (and ten cents wasn't going to cover that dental bill) and Johnny swallowed a quarter, reporting during show and tell two days later, much to your teacher's discomfort, that it had made its way safely through his digestive system and he didn't know why his mom wouldn't let him keep it. How could you forget the shining blue bicycle from Canadian Tire hidden in the trunk of the car or the birthday your parents found out your grandma had been diagnosed with cancer?

As we age, the tendency moves from trying to remember our birthdays to struggling to forget them. But even if we succeed in forgetting, time doesn't.

Acceptance seems to be the best bet, although I'm reluctant to accept this. There's nothing we can do about the passage of time. It's out of our hands. It lies in God's.

But perhaps there is a way we can take some control. We can choose what to do in that swift-moving flow of time. Who knows? We may end up using wisely, creatively, and thankfully the time granted us by the Creator. In any case, we can always look at it this way: we'll never again be as young as we are right now, so enjoy!

You are never too old to set another goal or to dream a new dream.

— Les Brown

Path Books
A LIGHT TO MY PATH

We hope that you have enjoyed reading this Path Book. For more information about Path Books, please visit our website at **www.pathbooks.com**. If you have comments or suggestions about Path Books, please write us at publisher@pathbooks.com.

Other Path Books

Christ Wisdom: Spiritual Practice in the Beatitudes and the Lord's Prayer *by Christopher Page*. The Beatitudes and the Lord's Prayer offer us a profound challenge to live in intimate communion with God. This pastorally-oriented book aims to help us discover new insights in Jesus' teaching. Each chapter includes reflective questions and spiritual exercises to help integrate the teachings into everyday life. *1-55126-420-X $16.95*

Oceans of Grief and Healing Waters: A Story of Loss and Recovery *by Marian Jean Haggerty*. With courageous candour and strength, Marian Haggerty tells the story of her journey toward healing from grief, after the death of a loved one. This book can be a wonderful companion for those who are alone and grieving, helping them to understand that they do not journey by themselves. *1-55126-396-3 $16.95*

Passiontide: A Novel *by Brian E. Pearson.* In the midst of a spirited West Coast people, David, an Anglican priest, veers into the tangled realms of love and passion, and stares even into the jaws of death. This unpredictable pilgrimage of the soul makes no guarantees and offers no safe haven. He will never be the same again.
1-55126-350-5 $24.95

How the Light Gets In: A Collection of Short Stories *by Brian E. Pearson.* In this sparkling collection, we glimpse the humour and humanity of a church preparing to enter its third millennium. The stories combine a real love of the church with a clear look at its foibles. They will touch the heart as well as the funny bone.
1-55126-258-4 $22.95

Practical Prayer: Making Space for God in Everyday Life *by Anne Tanner.* A richly textured presentation of the history, practices, and implications of Christian prayer and meditation to help people live a rewarding life in a stressful world.
1-55126-321-1 $18.95
Meditation CD: 1-55126-348-3 $18.95
Audio cassette: 1-55126-349-1 $16.95
Leader's Guide: 1-55126-347-5 $18.95

Healing Through Prayer: Health Practitioners Tell the Story *by Larry Dossey, Herbert Benson, John Polkinghorne, and others.* Prayer is powerful. In this unique book and video, doctors and patients quote scientific surveys and relate personal experiences of healing through prayer. They provide new conviction to people of faith, and new hope to those seeking healing.
1-55126-229-0 $18.95
The Power Within, one-hour video
1-55126-234-7 $29.95

God with Us: The Companionship of Jesus in the Challenges of Life *by Herbert O'Driscoll.* In thirty-three perceptive meditations, Herbert O'Driscoll considers the challenges of being human, searches key events in the life of Jesus, and discovers new vitality and guidance for our living. He shows us how the healing wisdom and power of Jesus' life can transform our own lives today.
1-55126-359-9 $18.95

Available from your local bookstore or
Anglican Book Centre, phone 1-800-268-1168
or write 80 Hayden Street, Toronto, ON M4Y 3G2.